Presented to the Westmar
College Library on the
occasion of the York
Reunion, 1982 — my 30th
anniversary!!

With fond remembrances
of York days, '50 to '52,
and Westmar days, as Chaplain,
'64 to '68.

Hal W. French

RELIGIOUS FERMENT IN MODERN INDIA

RELIGIOUS FERMENT IN MODERN INDIA

HAL W. FRENCH
and
ARVIND SHARMA

ST. MARTIN'S PRESS   NEW YORK

© Hal W. French and Arvind Sharma 1981

All rights reserved. For information, write:
St. Martin's Press, Inc. 175 Fifth Avenue, New York, N.Y, 10010
Printed in India
First Published in the United States of America in 1981

ISBN 0-312-67134-2

Library of Congress Cataloging in Publication Data

French, Hal W.
    Religious ferment in modern India
    Includes bibliographical references
    1. India—Religion, I. Sharma, Arvind

II. Title
BL20001.2F73   1981   294   81-5725
ISBN 0-312-67134-2   A ACR 2

CONTENTS

PREFACE

The book you intend to read deals with religious ferment in modern India. It is dualistic in several ways. It is the work of two authors, one American, the other Indian; they work on two continents, one on the American the other on the Australian; and they work formally with two different historical periods of Indian history—the modern and the ancient. Although thus dualistic in origin and structure, the book is single-minded (one almost said monistic) in intent. It seeks to provide the reader with a simple, perhaps even a simplified, introduction to the causes, course and consequences of religious ferment in modern India. It does not claim to be an exhaustive or encyclopaedic work, though it does try to be comprehensive. It aims at pointing out the territory and its high points and salient features to the reader rather than furnishing him with a map thereof.

Authors often feel called upon to justify their enterprise before a bar constituted of the anonymous but very real academics who ask, in subdued tones, in the galleries of the departments and over the dining-tables at conferences: why this book? The present authors are about to succumb to the urge to answer this question.

It is our feeling that the issues involved in the relationship of religion and politics in modern India are of much greater moment than the generally available books on the subject seem to indicate. True this is a book about modern and not contemporary India, where by modern is meant the period of Indian history stretching roughly from A.D. 1800 to 1947. But the contemporary rides on the shoulders of the modern. And modern India was fundamentally distinguished by two features which were really two sides of the same coin: the introduction of Western influences in India under the British Raj and the reaction to it on the part of the Indians. It is the interaction of these forces which shaped the history of the period. Nowhere was the interaction more pronounced than in the sphere of religion, which provides the focus of the present study.

Sometimes there is a danger, in the context of ancient India, of thinking about it uni-dimensionally and almost exclusively in terms of religion. There is a similar danger, in the context of modern India, of talking about it almost entirely in the political idiom. But while the neglect of the political element in ancient India may only imperil sound scholarship about the past, the neglect of the religious factor in the politics of modern India could have graver consequences. Ever since the Partition of the country the religious factor has remained a skeleton in the family cupboard, whose ghost continues to haunt the study of modern India, a ghost which often materializes in sanguinary ectoplasm, and a ghost which people are more concerned with exorcising than with examining. In this context the thesis of this book should be of some interest, namely, that modern India was a period of religious ferment which was spiritually, cultur-ally and politically consequential. The thesis is not novel; what the authors hope is new is its presentation with clarity and con-centration, with an eye on the general reader and the college and university student. After all, the British presence in India was a leaven which produced on the one hand a religious fer-ment out of which was distilled the heady wine of religious and political nationalism and on the other hand raised the dough which was kneaded into at least some of the repasts which appeared on the imperial table and the crumbs that fell from it. If this gastronomic metaphor has whetted the reader's appetite to read on then it has served its purpose.

One of us (AS) would take this opportunity of expressing thanks to my students, especially to those in my tutorials. Whether they learnt anything from me may be doubted but I owe much to them—this is certain in an otherwise uncertain world.

30. 6. 1981

HAL W. FRENCH
ARVIND SHARMA

by
Hal W. French

Introduction

The year 1757 often marks the beginning of what historians of the Indian scene have termed the British Period, or Modern India. Dates and labels are always arbitrary and misleading; so with these. The Battle of Plassey did seem to establish British supremacy, but not absolutely as ruling power by any means. The preceding period, similarly, may be called the Mughal Period, but the final years of the last of the Great Mughals, Aurangzeb, were characterized by erosion of his base of power, rapidly to be accentuated following his death in 1707. The English were one of the European rivals on the scene for well over a century before Plassey, so no clear demarcation can be of more than forensic utility. More than this, the designation of a period of history by the dominant ruling power is to accept a primarily political designation, also. The British were an enormously influential catalyst, however, in cultural and religious matters, so the wider accuracy of the label may be argued with some persuasiveness. Still, things Indian persisted. Social institutions, apparently vulnerable to attack through their lack of a center, proved amazingly durable.

It would be wrong to attribute this durability chiefly to intransigence to change. Two other qualities would seem to characterize the Indian milieu with more accuracy. Resilience and adaptibility describe the force of the Tradition. Reform and revival movements grew out of the mother lode. The period under consideration, then, is a profoundly Indian period. While we may with hesitation employ the customary terms, the alien label does distort. The sleeping giant is energized, new departures are witnessed, some of which initially appear to "ape the British." Those which remain, however, are of the soil, a revitalization of primal wisdom.

The focus of my research on India in the last ten years has been on such new and lively movements, those chiefly in the late nineteenth century which make up what has been termed The Indian Renaissance. It was a time of ferment, and beyond the initial catalyzing presence, the initiatives for change came much more from the Indian leaders themselves than from the British. This was evident even in the nineteenth century, particularly after the Mutiny of 1857. The religious movement to which I've given greatest attention prior to this book has been the Ramakrishna Movement. I am grateful to Kennikat Press, Port Washington, New York, for their permission to use materials from my book, *The Swan's Wide Waters*: *Ramakrishna and Western Culture*, rather extensively as the basis for Chapter Four of Part One here. With this acknowledgement here, I have not cited that book directly in the footnotes to Chapter Four. Similarly with the Sixth Chapter; some of that material first appeared in another format in an article, "Anagarika Dharmapala: Buddhist Revivalist and Ecumenist," in *Bengal*: *Studies in Literature, Society and History*, published in 1976 by Michigan State University. With these exceptions, materials for this book were gathered chiefly in the summer of 1975 in England and libraries in the Eastern United States and in Western U.S. and India on a sabbatical leave in the fall of 1978. They have not appeared elsewhere.

Amongmany others to whom gratitude could here be expressed, one name deserves particular mention. I spent a very pleasant and profitable week at the International Headquarters of the Theosophical Society in Adyar, south of Madras. The acting head of the Society, Dr. Jean Raymond, most graciously assisted my research, giving me access to the Society's archives, etc. I received word in May of this year, 1980, that she had just died, tragically, of rabies. The few pages on the Theosophical Society in Chapter Three are dedicated to her for her singular helpfulness.

A wider word of dedication is offered to my father, deceased in 1975, and to my mother. Thoroughly committed to the Christian enterprise, it has demanded something of them to see their son's major researches taking him into other cultures and faiths. But they have taken pride in that, sought to understand my own fascination with it, and have been unfailingly supportive.

India and the British till 1813
Reasons for the British Presence

A curious quotation resides at the top of one of eight large columns around the main reading room of the Library of Congress in Washington. "We taste the spices of Arabia," it reads, "yet never feel the scorching sun that brings them forth." The patent point of the quotation would seem to be polemic against luxury and indolence. The curiosity lies, however, in the contrasting intent of the anonymous author, whose obscure book, *Considerations Upon the East India Trade*, was first published in 1701. He was waxing eloquent in this passage about the advantages of foreign trade to Britain. "Why," he asks, "are we surrounded by the sea? Surely that our wants at home might be supplied by our navigation with other countries, the least and easiest labour. By this we taste the spices of Arabia, yet we never feel the scorching sun that brings them forth. We shine in silks which our hands have not wrought . . . we only plough the deep and reap the harvest of every country in the world."[1]

The author was perhaps the first competent advocate of free trade, anticipating Adam Smith and Josiah Tucker in their critique of classic mercantile theory, with its protective restrictions for the supposed benefit of British commercial interests. Free trade advocates opposed tariffs and quotas, and monopolistic arrangements with colonies. Later this position was to call into question the economic value to Britain of her whole

---

[1]P.J. Thomas, *Mercantilism and the East India Trade* (London: Frank Cass Co., 1926), p. 91.

colonial system, but this is to anticipate. Here it is necessary to note that supporters of both theories felt that their policies would bring greatest gain to Britain. Thus we begin with the obvious: the primary rationale for the British presence in India was economic. The wealth of the East, through trading, could be secured with minimal effort and expenditure to the people of Britain.

A. THE MERCANTILE INCENTIVE

First chartered by Queen Elizabeth in 1600, the British East India Company for over 150 years could not properly be said to have entertained imperialistic ambitions. Along with merchant fleets from other European nations, English vessels sailed to load themselves with the treasures of the Orient, not to conquer, to settle and to govern Asian territories. Such power as they wielded was to secure their trading interests. In the islands of Indonesia, the source of the most highly valued Asian commodity, spices, the British proved early to have too little power. Suffering a crushing defeat at the hands of the Dutch in 1623, the Company turned northward to what it regarded as a second best area for exploitation, India. Here there was little open confrontation till the middle of the 18th century, either with existing powers in India or from rival European forces, the Danish, the Portuguese and the French. Each of the European nations desired nothing more than a little secure space around a few ports through which trade might funnel. For the British, these mercantile deltas emerged at Madras, Bombay and, most importantly, Calcutta.

While Mughal rule was dominant, and while conflicts in Europe did not seriously extend the threat of confrontation between the same powers, the separate national companies could pursue their interests relatively unmolested. The Western presence was not perceived as ominous while the Mughals themselves were strong. There were those in the courts of Akbar and Jahangir who objected to the first of the Westerners on religious grounds, but the prevailing mood of the court was catholic, open to all of the fresh winds of culture and change. Jahangir could be enormously vexing and vacillating to early representatives such as Roe and Hawkins, but the men were ingenious and persevering, and their beachhead held.

The later Mughals, Shah Jehan and Aurangzeb, were less hospitable, but the defeat of the latter brought an instability which was still more distressing. The power vacuum which followed forced the British out of their tiny European settlements in the forts at their three central outposts. A modicum of stability had to be forged if trade were to continue, and no indigenous force seemed likely to provide it. Here, then, were the first intimations of what would be felt as a mandate for rule, not merely trade. It was zealously resisted by the practical businessmen who came for profit. Even for them, though, the imperative grew more apparent. The Mughals were in disarray as effective rulers; despite their formidable mastery over nearly two centuries, they had retained an alien quality which made them vulnerable to perpetual challenge. But such challenges as could be mounted, from such groups as the Marathas, for example, could not promise stable government and public order. Leaders like Shivaji could mobilize religious and incipient nationalistic ardor in response to the Muslim fanaticism of Aurangzeb, but they had no true political skills nor ambitions. Hinduism itself, which might, we imagine, have provided some organizing facility, was not constituted to do so for lack of a center. Its fortunes, from centuries of rule by Muslim conquerors, were particularly at low ebb during this period, also, and the reformer's voice from within was sorely needed. As Pandit vidyasagar could lament in the middle of the nineteenth century, and Vivekananda later, local customs were the only visible authority. These were inviolate, impervious to change, protective of gross social inequity. "What a mighty influence is thine, O custom . . . Thou hast trampled over the Shastras, triumphed over virtue, and crushed the power of discriminating right from wrong and good from evil!"[2] If it were true in the mid-nineteenth century, when Vidyasagar opposed the intransigence of his society, it was doubly so a century before the times of such reformers.

But the mind of Britain, so long as it could be maintained, was for a policy of non-interference with local custom and no

---

[2]Ishwarchandra Vidyasagar, *Marriage of Hindu Widows* (Calcutta: K.P. Bagchi, 1975), pp. 107, 108.

expansion of territorial holdings. Thomas Roe, first ambassa-
dor to the Mughal court, had counseled this policy; clear
advantages seemed to favor its continuance for a time. A low
profile, non-intrusive presence seemed best calculated to serve
British mercantile interests. Circumstances, however, were to
dictate expedient lapses from this stance until it had to be
abandoned altogether. Coupled with political instability
throughout India, the European powers found that wars at
home exacerbated tensions in the colonies; India became yet
another battleground for the playing out of these national rival-
ries. This became particularly intense between the East India
Companies of Great Britain and France during the war of
Austrian Succession. In 1746, the French, pitted against the
English in Europe, sanctioned raids on English commerce on
the southeast coast of India. Dupleix, the new Governor-general, however, enlarged it into a full-scale operation resulting in
the capture of Madras by the French. Although this was yielded after a few years by European treaty, Dupleix continued to
solidify his position by alliances with native rulers in the Carnatic,
till his defeat by an adventurous young clerk. This man, Robert
Clive, swiftly mustered an army to seize Arcot, the Carnatic
capital, while the French army was out foraging. When they
returned he held his trophy under siege till help arrived, and
overnight became the man of the hour for the British. Called on
in another emergency situation in Bengal, he again defeated the
French forces at Chandernagore and won the highly significant
battle of Plassey, north of Calcutta in 1757. This, actually a
triumph of field diplomacy more than a pitched battle, has often
been cited as the event that marked England's claim to dominance in the sub-continent. The French were in eclipse in India,
a fact confirmed by the Treaty of Paris in 1763, and the various
competing native powers now had, increasingly, to come to
terms with the British.

There was, however, no instant transition by officers of the
British East India Company from men in pursuit of profit to
wise and benevolent rulers. Clive and others following his
example, traded privately, accepted lucrative favors, etc., until
their conduct became a scandal to London and change was
demanded. Reform, it was felt, could best be effected through
centralization, and this was done by unifying the three presi-

dencies under a Governor-general in Calcutta. Parliament's decision was implemented better than they knew in the selection of Warren Hastings to fill this position. Less under the necessity of his predecessors to maintain the fiction of rule by the Nawab with ever stronger support, he had more of a feeling for the native codes and customs by which the country might be ruled than did his successors. In other words, he assumed the mantle of power as was necessary, yet without the imposition of alien structures with which the rulers might be more comfortable. The movement from profit to administration required a transition from trading to taxing as a primary support base, for instance. But whereas Hastings had a strong feeling for the *ryots* or small, landholding peasants, his successor, Lord Cornwallis, appointed in 1786, was uncomfortable with the absence of a class of large landholders such as existed in Britain. To simplify the collection of taxes and to provide a more stable base, then, he created in Bengal the function of tax farmer for the *zamindars*, who supervised the gathering of fixed revenues from the operators of the land. In effect, their own percentage of these revenues rendered them in a better position than owner, unsubject to the vagaries of drought and monsoon for their income.

The very title given to Cornwallis' act, The Permanent Settlement, acknowledged that by this time the British had assumed what those terms convey, i.e., the right and responsibility to make such ordinances as would provide for public order for the foreseeable future. It was a still reluctant claim, and men such as Lord Cavendish more than once voiced an opinion widely shared, saying, he "wished to God every European could be extirpated from India and the country resorted to merely on the principles of commerce."[3] But the purely mercantile presence could no longer be sustained; by the end of the century a clear consensus had emerged that "Rule, Britannia," must in some measure be effected. Given such consensus, what were the influences which determined how English governance would be shaped in India?

[3]Vincent T. Harlow, *The Founding of the Second British Empire, 1763—1793*, vol. 2 (London: Longmans, Green and Co., 1964).

B. Utilitarian Philosophy

This movement, articulated by men such as Jeremy Bentham, James Mill and his son, John Stuart Mill, was clearly a major force in determining British policy. While none of these men ever visited India, the careers of the Mills in particular were closely linked with that country, the father through the publication of his massive *History of India*, and both through long association with the East India Company as officers. Interestingly, one of the earliest and most concise statements of Utilitarian principles was made by Richard Wellesley, the Governor-general whose aggressive policies forced the English conscience to develop a rationale for its expanded rule in India. Wellesley, who succeeded Cornwallis in 1798, moved to an expansionist policy almost immediately. Although the directors of the Company were extremely chary of anyone with territorial ambitions, the chairman, Henry Dundas, also oriented from his position as War Minister, supported such ambitions on the part of Wellesley. By now the dominant power in India for some time, England still had troublesome native rivals. In addition, the threat was newly posed that the French had ambitions toward India once more. Napoleon's navies had sailed through the Mediterranean and moved into Egypt with an army. Rumors were rampant that he might form an alliance with certain of the disaffected Indian states, and this, it was felt, must be forestalled. A clear military victory over Tipu in the south, the division of Maratha powers, treaties in the heartland and north of India advantageous to England, with the formation of subsidiary alliances, followed under Wellesley in the next few years. The British, one among several claimants for supremacy in 1798, were unchallenged as the paramount power in the subcontinent by 1805, when Wellesley left India.

Wellesley's statement to the directors of the East India Company on July 9, 1800, was as follows: "We feel that it would not only be unpolitic, but highly immoral to suppose that Providence has admitted of the establishment of British power over the finest provinces of India, with any other view than that of its being conducive to the happiness of the people, as well as to

our national advantage."[4] The teaching of a reciprocal good
in which all participating parties prosper is basic to Utilitarian
thought, although the sanctioning of policy by supposedly
known Providential purpose is more reminiscent of Adam Smith
than the more secular Utilitarian position. Smith invoked the
"invisible hand" to explain the manner in which trading
interests, devoted to the profit of those pursuing them, often
work to bring benefits to others. "By pursuing his own interest
he frequently promotes that of the society more effectually than
when he really intends to promote it."[5] The Utilitarians were
less confident that a kindly Providence would overrule man's
selfish ends to effect the general good, and advocated a more
directly intentional concern for humanitarian goals. Smith's
position could soothe the conscience of the exploiter; curiously,
the more secular position, which did not invoke the "Divine
plan," seems better to have engaged Englishmen in responsible
action toward India, not attached to private gain.

John Stuart Mill, in citing influences from his father, says of
him, "He found it impossible to believe that a world so full of
evil was the work of an Author combining infinite power with
perfect goodness and righteousness."[6] Such a belief, James
Mill was persuaded, was the greatest enemy of morality, in
that it vitiated the existing order of things as a fatally conve-
nient pretext for moral lassitude. J.S. Mill says of himself, then,
"I am thus one of the very few examples, in this country, of
one who has, not thrown off religious belief, but never had it:
I grew up in a negative state with regard to it."[7] Yet he could
counterpoise the "Religion of Humanity," devoid of supernatural sanctions from a god of dubious morality, as a force which
would genuinely engage men in caring relationships.[8] This, he
felt, was what Utilitarian philosophy had to offer to the world,

[4]Ramsay Muir, *The Making of British India*, Manchester: The
University Press, 1923), p. 246.

[5]Adam Smith, *"Wealth of Nations* (New York: The Modern
Library, 1937), p. 243.

[6]John Stuart Mill, *Autobiography*, (New York: Henry Holt and
Co., 1873), p. 41.

[7]Ibid., p. 43.

[8]J.S. Mill, *Nature and Utility of Religion and Theism* (London:
Longmans, Green, Reader and Dyer, 1874), pp. 69-122.

and what, from his own long career orientation, he sought to offer to India. The Utilitarian position became a support base for enlightened intervention and reform measures. As private trade interests were allowed to share in the Company's earlier monopolistic commercial pursuits, and as the Company itself was forced, ultimately, in 1833, to become solely an administrative entity, it was necessary that an operative philosophy of concern for the welfare of India be visible. This the Utilitarians provided and as we shall see, crucial policy decisions were implemented because of it. Although Utilitarianism has often been maligned and equated with expediency, two examples may serve to modify that caricature. One, in devising legal codes for India, the Utilitarians did not seek merely to adapt British legal precedents to local circumstances. They saw themselves as independent of legal models from any country, seeking rather to implement insights from the universal science of jurisprudence. This is most clear in the Penal Code drafted by Macaulay in 1835, where innovation was more possible than with civil law, where vested property rights, etc., were involved. Bentham's principles for what such a code should embody, and which Macaulay sought to apply, stated that punishment should be "variable, equable, commensurable, characteristic of the offense, exemplary, frugal, subservient to reformation, popular, simple and remissible."[9] The second example indicates that the Utilitarian contribution was not monolithic in all cases, nor was it impervious to change. John Stuart Mill later modified the position of his predecessors, in valuing liberty more highly. For him, representative self-government came to be viewed as essential, and he could hold that good government was no substitute for self-government. This must certainly be seen as a significant departure from the paternalistic implications of "the greatest good for the greatest number," the phrase most often employed to encapsulate Utilitarian philosophy.

C. THE EVANGELICALS

The Evangelical Movement was another powerful force for

---

[9] Eric Stokes, *The English Utilitarians and India* (Oxford: Oxford University Press, 1959), p. 231.

change in India. A number of missionaries may be named among them, but the primary impetus for this movement came from a long-time Company servant, Charles Grant, upon his return from India. Ainslee Embree has detailed the circumstances of Grant's personal spiritual revolution in India in 1776, and the consequent aversion which he came to feel for religious customs and practices of India's native religions.[10] Elected a director of the East India Company in 1794, four years after his return, he sought to gain permission for the sending of missionaries without the severe restrictions which had been operative. This followed his failure, the previous year, to secure the adoption of his "Pious Clause" in the renewal of the Company charter, where he was suggesting active government support of missionaries and teachers in India. The reluctance persisted, partly because of the colonial example in America, with the feeling that education coupled with missionary activity would lead to similar dissatisfaction in India. Grant was joined by such men as William Wilberforce and others who made up the Clapham Sect, and who advocated abolition of the slave trade as well. Christianity, for Grant, was to be the chief civilizing agent in the colonies, and in this the British, he said, "were called to imitate the Roman conquerors, who civilized and improved the nations whom they subdued."[11] The analogy is curious, but Grant was clear on what he felt to be British responsibility in this regard, and the manner in which its discharge would also enhance English commercial interests.

In considering the affairs of the world as under the control of the Supreme Disposer, and those distant territories. . .providentially put into our hands, is it not necessary to conclude that they were given to us, not merely that we might draw an annual profit from them, but that we might diffuse among their inhabitants, long sunk in darkness, vice and misery, the

[10]Ainslee Embree, *Charles Grant and British Rule in India* (New York: Columbia University Press, 1962), pp. 49—54.

[11]Thomas Fisher, *Memoir of the Late Charles Grant esq.* (London: J.L. Cox and Son, 1833), p. 28. The model of implementation by military force was likewise not particularly odious to the Utilitarian mind, with their congenital disposition for order, discipline and efficiency.

light and benign influence of the truth, the blessings of well-
regulated society, the improvements and comforts of active
industry? . . . In every progressive step to this work, we shall
also serve the original design with which we visited India,
that design still so important to this country—the extension
of our commerce.[12]

Grant was a zealous spokesman for the Evangelicals, who were
years, however, in being able successfully to promote their cause.
The intemperance of missionary publications inveighing against
the native faiths, reports that the Vellore Mutiny of 1807 was
stimulated by careless interference with religious practices, etc.,
made the directors reluctant to intrude in the Indian scene by
making it an open preserve for missionary activity. This, it was
felt, would be inflammatory. The Evangelicals, however, argued
that English education and the proclamation of Christianity
would promote the civilizing influences that again could cause
British interests to prosper. "In this way," it was held, "the
noblest species of conquest, the spread of true religion and
knowledge, would not forfeit its earthly reward; for wherever
our principles and our language are introduced, our commerce
will follow."[13] This may seem a blatant association, but it was
doubtless necessary to secure requisite support for the desired
legislation. Wilberforce effected a coalition of Christian groups
favorable to missionaries being allowed to enter India, and
sought in a long speech in Commons at the time of Charter
renewal in 1813 to prove that, "Our Christian religion is sublime, pure and beneficent. The Indian religious system is mean,
licentious and cruel . . . It is one grand abomination."[14] While
this was provocative of bitter debate, the Evangelicals had by
this time sufficient strength to secure passage, and missionaries
were regularly sent to India in the years following. The growing
Christian presence was to prove a powerful, if at times an
irritating and intolerant, catalyst for social change. Earlier
Catholic missionaries, such as the Jesuit priest Robert de

[12]Stokes, op. cit., p. 34.
[13]Ibid.
[14]G.H. Philips, *The East India Company*, *1784-1834* (Manchester:
Manchester University Press, 1961), p. 191.

Nobili, had sought to divest the Gospel from its western cultural trappings, and were less threatening to established customs than this new breed. De Nobili, in fact, came under considerable ecclesiastical criticism for the way in which he acclimated himself to caste structures. He became extremely fluent in Sanskrit and southern vernacular languages and could engage in learned debates in the classical manner. His own priestly life was enhanced in the Indian scene with his assumption of Brahmin dress and life style.[15] Nineteenth century British Evangelical missionaries, however, were of a different temper, distinctly non-accommodative in tone.

It is important to note that the missionary's victory was not complete, even so. The official Company's "attitude toward Hindu and Moslem religions was that of patron or protector."[16] This involved support, tacit and specific, through the management of temples, the collecting of taxes, repair of temples and their precincts, the firing of salutes at festival processions, etc. All of this was anathema to the missionaries, who caricatured the British as having become "church-wardens of Juggernaut and dry nurses of Vishnu."[17] It was not enough, from the Christian perspective, to allow them access to India. The government must also cease and desist from its promotion of heathen activities.

D. THE ORIENTALISTS

One more factor of the English presence needs to be mentioned, this one a positive stimulus through the increased stature it gave to the traditions of India. The service rendered by these scholars, the Orientalists, to the cultural heritage of India is scarcely subject to overtones of imperialism in any form.

[15]See S. Rajamaniakam, ed., *Roberto de Nobili on Indian Customs* Palayamkottai: (De Nobili Research Institute, 1972), passim; and Michael Foss, *The Founding of the Jesuits* (London: Hamish Hamilton, 1969), pp. 217 ff.

[16]Romesh Chandra Benerjee, "State Patronage to Hindu and Muslim Religions During the East India Company's Rule," *Bengal Past and Present*, LVI, January to June, 1939, 23 —36.

[17]Stephen Neill, *The Story of Christian Church in India and Pakistan* (Grand Repids: Eerdman's 1970).

Foremost among them was also the earliest significant one after
de Nobili, Sir William Jones, who under the sympathetic support
of Warren Hastings, brought his phenomenal linguistic skills to
the study of Sanskrit. Already a master of Latin, Greek and
Persian, he could approach its structure and syntax comparatively.
But he did more than the necessary analytic task; he became a
translator and profound appreciator of the cultural heritage of
India. His was more than a single scholar's efforts, also. In
working to infuse new life into the Asiatic Society, he insured
that his efforts would survive his death in 1794. Others, such as
Wilkins, Colebrooke, and H.H. Wilson made their own contributions, as did William Carey, the latter from the standpoint of
missionary persuasion. Originally beginning his studies of the
vernaculars (rather than Sanskrit), to facilitate translations of
Scriptures in spreading the Gospel, Carey came to have a great
feeling for the life of the common people, to which his knowledge of their language gave him access. In his *Dialogues*
(Kathopakathan), composed as a Bengali reader for his Fort
William students, Carey in fact produced a document of
intense social significance. David Kopf, referring to S.K. De's
research on this book, says of it, "It was the first book by a
European that did not concern itself with high Hindu culture.
For the first time the idiomatic language, manners, and customs
of merchants, fishermen, women, beggars, day-laborers, and
other common folk were given the dignity of 'minute and
sympathetic attention.' It would not be far-fetched to call
Carey, as a result of this work alone, India's first cultural
anthropologist."[18]

While most scholars, in retrospect, would credit the Orientalists with great achievements in the Indian Renaissance, Kopf
goes further in his valuable work, making the case that Sanskrit
and the vernaculars could, indeed, have been vehicles of
modernization had the Orientalists won the day. He questions,
also, the reforms effected by law, by Bentinck, Macaulay, and
other English rulers, as essentially intrusive as well, and credits
the opposition to these with more integrity and feeling for
India's own necessary rhythms than is usual. An assessment of

---

[18]David Kopf, *British Orientalism and the Bengal Renaissance*
(Barkeley: University of California Press, 1969), p. 93.

this position is beyond our province here, but we should attempt to isolate briefly the forces which obviated a full application of Orientalist policy. Here it is the father, James Mill, not the more philosophically illustrious son, who was the prime mover. In his *History of British India* Mill reserved his most virulent attacks for Sir William Jones, regarding his feeling for the stature of Asian society as credulous and romantic. Speaking of his views on the Arabs, but similarly for the Hindus, Mill could say, "The rhapsodies of Rousseau on the virtue and happiness of the savage life surpass not the panegyrics of Sir William."[19] This had, for Mill, a very real and negative practical effect. "Sir William Jones and others," he writes, "recognized the demand for a code of Indian law; but unhappily thought of no better expedient than that of employing some of the natives themselves; as if one of the most difficult tasks to which the human mind can be applied, a work to which the highest measure of European intelligence is not more than equal, could be expected to be tolerably performed by the unenlightened and perverted intelligence of a few Indian pundits."[20] Mill's patent chauvinism extended, also, to his assessment of Sanskrit, whose sophistication, again, he felt to have been romanticized by Jones and other Orientalists. Appalled, for instance, that the language could have twenty words for the same object, the sun, this was judged redundancy, superfluity, "frivolous refinements which are suited to the taste of an uncivilized people."[21] The principle of utility, for Mill, should require simplicity and precision instead.

The attempt, in this initial chapter, has been to isolate the varied perspectives from which British policy makers operated. Considerable consensus was able to be forged between the first three, those representing the interests of the merchant, the Utilitarian philosophers and the Evangelicals, as we shall explore. The Orientalists clearly had some conclusions which were unassimilable with the political directions of the others, but the strategies and goals of each of the four could be profiled

[19]James Mill, *The History of British India* (Chicago: University of Chicago Press, 1975), p. 229.
[20]Ibid., pp. 555, 556.
[21]Ibid., p. 209.

with some clarity by 1813. The Charter was renewed, and a chief reform measure, the opening of British India to missionaries, would soon cause dramatic action/reaction on the Indian scene.

| British and Indian Initiatives
in Reform, 1813-1857

A. HARMONIZING OF BRITISH INTERESTS

Macaulay, writing in the 1830s, summed up the new consensus
which began to shape British policy toward India after 1813. "It
is scarcely possible," he wrote, "to calculate the benefits which
we might derive from the diffusion of European civilization
among the vast population of the East. . ." From this followed
his cogent premise : "To trade with civilized men is infinitely
more profitable than to govern savages."[1] Britain needed, by
this time, not merely a source of raw materials for her industries
but a wider market for her manufactured goods. This, for
economic reasons, dictated different strategies toward colonies
such as India. No longer a non-intrusive presence, a reluctant
rule, but a willingness now was evidenced to modify the structures of Indian society. The civilizing of the Indian people
meant, for economic interests, the cultivation in their midst of
English tastes and appetites. Even a rough carbon culture of
England in the East could mean a vast new market for English
commodities. How was this to be effected? The twin arm of
English education and the Christian Gospel were ready to be
employed for the civilizing, or better, Europeanizing, task. And
in the first of these, the Evangelicals often worked in tandem
with Utilitarians to effect reform. As Percival Spear notes, the
Utilitarians had "a faith in reason as strong as the Evangelical
confidence in the Gospel."[2] Thus we see men such as Macaulay

[1]Stokes, op. cit., p. 44.
[2]Percival Spear, *A History of India*, vol. 2 (Baltimore: Penguin
Books, 1965), p. 122.

and Alexander Duff implementing the idea that the English
language might be a strong vehicle for modernity in India, the
former acting out of Utilitarian principles, the other from his
strong Scottish Calvinist traditions. Grant again, a generation
and more earlier, had argued first, that the Company's business
and administrative affairs should all be conducted in English, then
that this would not only improve its managerial efficiency, but
"through its use the natives would inevitably learn the arts,
philosophy and religion of the governing race, and 'the fabric
of error' would be silently undermined. English education
would not only affect the opinions and beliefs of the upper
classes but it would also reach down to the peasant bound to
poverty by his 'diminutive plough' and 'miserable cattle.'"[3] The
case for English remained, for some, closely tied with the proclamation of Christianity, as Grant had proposed earlier in his
'Pious Clause'. Macaulay could reflect this, also, in writing to
his devout father a year after the passage of his famous Education Minute in 1835, stating his firm belief that if the program
for English education were pursued, there would not be a single
idolater among the respectable classes in Bengal thirty years
later."[4] The same extravagant hopes were still being voiced far
beyond the thirty years, that a core of "enlightened Hindus"
accepting Christianity was prophetic of the nation's turning.
In 1902 the editor of *The Calcutta Review* expressed his strong
belief that the process of Christianization of India was well
underway, through the embracing to Christ of "the most earnest
seeker. . . the moral heroes. . .who are the real salt, strength,
stamina of the nation. . .When these," he confidently predicted,
"have all been gathered into the Christian Church, the rest of
the wavering and the careless, even though in the vast majority,
will follow as a matter of course."[5]

If this optimism was unjustified, the Christian presence still
constituted a formidable challenge, as did the total program of
education through the English medium. Consider again
Macaulay's above quoted statement: "To trade with civilized

[3]Embree, op. cit., p. 151.
[4]Stokes, op. cit., pp. 45, 46.
[5]Editorial, "The Quarter", *Calcutta Review*, vol. 114, April, 1902,
p. 399.

men is infinitely more profitable than to govern savages."
Though this seems crass, and despite Macaulay's arrogant confidence in the superiority of British culture, the Indian historian
and diplomat K.M. Pannikar has called his Education Minute
the most beneficently revolutionary decision taken by the British
government in India. "It is the genius of this man, narrow in
his Europeanism, self-satisfied in his sense of English greatness,
that gives life to modern India as we know it."[6] This is high
tribute, and it may be paid, not alone to an "invisible hand"
behind the selfish motives of some of the British in India, but to
the clear intentionality of others. Among the latter would rank
William Bentinck, whose abolition of *sati*, the immolation of
Hindu widows on the funeral pyres of their husbands, paved the
way for other needed social legislation. India did need such
reforms, and certain among the English leaders till the time of
the Great Mutiny in 1857, were courageous in implementing
them. Similarly with the total Christian presence; although, as
acknowledged it could prove an irritant under the Indian
societal skin, in its stimulation of social reform, as K. Natarajan,
editor of *The Indian Social Reformer*, has recognized, "The fear
of the Christian missionary has been the beginning of much
social wisdom among us."[7] While the anticipated 'turning to
Christ' did not occur in terms of mass conversions, other efforts,
such as the opening of schools and hospitals, the championing
of the rights of women, widows in particular, quickened the
conscience of Hinduism. From within the bosom of Bharat
Mata, Mother India, renewal began to emerge.

B. THE FIRST MODERN INDIAN REFORMER:
RAJA RAMMOHUN ROY

The first name to be considered among modern Indian reformers
must certainly be that of Raja Rammohun Roy, rightfully
accorded such ascriptions as "the Father of Modern India,"
"The first really cosmopolitan type in India," "Pioneer of
Modern Indian Renaissance," etc. The range of his inquiries

[6]Sir Percival Griffiths, *The British Impact on India* (London:
McDonald, 1952), p. 250.

[7]Charles Heimsath, *Indian Nationalism and Hindu Social Reform*
(Princeton: Princeton University Press, 1964), p. 53.

even as a child could not be satisfied within a narrow sphere. Hinduism, as he encountered it, seemed resistant to change, decadent in its idolatrous and superstitious practices. He was initially exposed to wider influences through a study of Persian in his native village and then at Patna, a famous seat of Muslim learning. This education deepened his maturing convictions about the need for religious reform. As he began, both verbally and in print, to express his thoughts while still a teenager, relations with family and friends became strained so that he was forced to leave home for a time. "He was banished from his father's house once or twice; he was insulted by his friends; his life was threatened, and even in the streets of Calcutta he had to walk about armed. Later in his life his relations (his own mother) tried to deprive him of his caste, and indirectly of his property."[8]

Roy began a thorough study of Vedic sources to try to make his case for a purer ancient model of Indian religion. He translated and published five of the Upanishads in 1816 and 1817, with comments, to support his claim that true Hinduism was monotheistic and highly ethical. On practical grounds as well he stated, in *Defence of Hindoo Theism*, his objections to current religious practices. He suggested that the worship of Krishna encouraged nudity, debauchery and murder. The worship of Kali, he said, was characterized by intoxication, criminal intercourse, and licentious songs. Contemporary Hindu idolatry, he argued, destroyed the texture of society "more than any other pagan worship."[9]

Roy was nevertheless not persuaded to sever his own roots in Hinduism and the Brahmin caste to adopt either Islam or Christianity. He sought, in fact, to be a critic of those religions as well. He had begun contact with the Serampore missionaries as early as 1816, and in 1820 he crowned his critical study of the New Testament with the publication of *Precepts of Jesus, The Guide to Peace and Happiness*. In this he sought to make available to his countrymen the moral teachings of Jesus,

[8]F. Max Muller, *I Point to India*, ed. by Nanda Mookerjee (Bombay Shakuntala Publishing House, 1970), p. 41.

[9]Rammohun Roy, *The English Works of Rammohun Roy*, vol. 2, ed., by Kalidas Nag and Debajyoti Burman (Calcutta: Sadharan Brahmo Samaj. 1945—1951), pp. 60, 92.

because he felt that these teachings seemed more capable than any other of elevating human behavior and motivation. His efforts were not appreciated by the men of Serampore, however, and Marshman, in particular, began a series of critical responses which attacked him for his separation of Jesus as ethical teacher from his identity as Son of God and Savior in the Gospels. Roy's response was to state that his primary purpose was to urge Christians to preach the simple and sublime moral truths of the Gospel and not to insist on assent to rigid dogmatic interpretations, belief in miracles, etc. He nevertheless remained for Marshman, "an intelligent Heathen, whose mind is as yet completely opposed to the grand design of the Savior's becoming incarnate."[10] Doctrinally, the only rapport that Roy subsequently enjoyed with the Serampore missionaries was with William Adam, who moved closer to a Unitarian position, and who worked with Roy later in the establishment of the Brahmo Samaj.

In areas of social concern, however, Roy held common cause with Evangelicals and Utilitarians alike on many issues. Chief among these were the promotion of English education and the abolition of *suttee* (*sati*). British records in the early 1820s indicated that *suttees* were increasing, despite the passage of local ordinances against the practice or through active interference, under guidelines such as "where the woman is unwilling or is under sixteen, or is pregnant, drugged or intoxicated, or has small children."[11] But there was no overall prohibition. The strategy of the British was largely that of opposition on the grounds of universal human rights. Roy sought to make his case primarily through a search of the Hindu sacred texts. His conclusion, first published in a tract in 1822, from many citations, was that, far from demanding *suttee*, ancient law provided for honorable maintenance of widows. Roy's researches on this subject provided a valuable premise for Bentinck's Minute of December 4, 1829, abolishing *suttee*, although Roy opposed direct legislation at the time, fearing an excessive outcry against the British. He helped to stem this, however, after the Minute

[10]Sophia Dobson Collet, *The Life and Letters of Raja Rammohun Roy* (Calcutta: Sadharan Brahmo Samaj, 1962), p. 115.
[11]Ibid , p. 81.

was issued. Orthodox opposition continued, but the practice
was discontinued almost overnight, and the consensus of scholarship appears to be that, while opposition to the British because
of this and other reform measures may have intensified, the
vitality of Hinduism certainly did not depend on such peripheral
and questionable practices.

Rammohun Roy was concerned to restore this vitality and,
in addition to this the pruning of Hinduism's lush vines of
decadent and idolatrous growth, he sought to create a model of
simple, theistic worship in fidelity to what he understood to be
Vedic insights. Dialogue was continued with the Unitarian
Association from which, with Adam's co-leadership, it had
grown, but this was more specifically Hindu and the purpose
was more clearly worship. The Unitarian pattern was useful,
since Hinduism had no developed model of congregational
worship, but the content was from the ancient Indian texts. The
service for the two evening hours consisted of the reading of the
Vedas, with explanation, a discourse in Bengali, then hymns,
sung with instrumental accompaniment. Roy's initial statement
claimed that the worship pattern of the Brahmo Samaj enshrined
the ancient and still most enlightened insight of his people. It
advocated "direct worship. . .attested by revelation (in Scrip-
ture), by reason, which discarded all outward ceremonies and
found worship to consist in self-discipline, self-realization, and
service of others, and by experience. . ."[12] Too austere for the
masses of Hindus, too specifically Indian in content for liberal
Europeans who were nevertheless benevolently disposed towards
it, it did provide a bridge to Hindu intellectuals for Roy, and
the comradeship with his countrymen which had been so long
denied him.

Although the Raja supported discriminating study of the
ancient sources of the Indian tradition, he definitely stood with
the Anglicists against the Orientalists on education generally.
Having assisted David Hare in the establishment of the Hindu
College, he opposed the opening of a Sanskrit college in Calcutta
as a retrogressive move. In a letter of protest he said, "The
Sanskrit language, so difficult that almost a lifetime is necessary
for its perfect acquisition, is well known to have been for ages

[12]Ibid., p. 225.

a lamentable check on the diffusion of knowledge; and the learning concealed under this impervious veil is far from sufficient to reward the labour of acquiring it. . . The Sanskrit system of education would be the best calculated to keep this country in darkness, if such had been the policy of the British legislature. . ."[13] Thus we witness Roy's support for Alexander Duff and others who had little regard for the culture and traditions of India, because of the tools of modernity which they could offer to India. Shortly after Duff arrived, Roy left for England to secure help for the reforms begun, and he died there in Bristol, shortly after the 1833 reform legislation was passed. His faith in the British hung in jeopardy while these measures were being uncertainly weighed, but he could write to a friend, William Rathbone, after their passage, "Thank Heaven, I can now feel proud of being one of your fellow subjects."[14]

C. ROY'S SUCCESSORS IN REFORM IN BENGAL

Roy's legacy in the Brahmo Samaj languished till Debendranath Tagore assumed its leadership in the 1840s, but he was more immediately succeeded in reform measures by followers of the Young Bengal Movement. Despite their feeling that Roy was too timid, this group continued some of his reform measures such as freedom of the press to a more successful conclusion, if in less decorous fashion. Clearly to the left of Roy, this Movement crystallized around one of the most controversial figures of the nineteenth century, Henry Louis Derozio. Much of the genius of this young teacher at the Hindu College in Calcutta lay in the methodology of free, informed discussion which he initiated, and in the spirit of free inquiry advocated by the sources which he shared with his students. The Movement continued after his dismissal and early death, despite the juvenile excesses of many of its members. The flaunting of their habits of eating beef and drinking wine before the orthodox left them in danger of total isolation as a small pocket of rabid rebels, but other, more sage counsels, also tutored them sympathetically. David Hare, who had opposed Derozio's dismissal, supported

[13]Griffiths, op. cit., p. 429.
[14]Collet, op. cit., p. 334.

most of their objectives and retained great influence among their members. While the Movement remained largely self-contained among the radical students of Hindu College, its members gradually matured and dispersed to become effective leaders in nineteenth century Bengal. Although it did not persist as a movement, an 1861 interpreter commented, "The youthful band of reformers who had been educated at the Hindoo College, like the tops of the Kanchenjunga, were the first to catch and reflect the dawn. . . . When has an opposition to popular prejudices been dissociated with difficulty and trouble?"[15] Thirty years earlier, after Derozio's death at age 23, the *Calcutta Gazette* paid him a tribute which might have foreshadowed the later assessment: "If his speculations were not always conclusive, or his inferences always legitimately formed, his moral character was irreproachable; his devotion to the spirit of what he deemed truth, even romantically uncompromising; his intentions unquestionably good."[16]

The more sober strains of devotion were resumed in the Brahmo Samaj in 1842, with the joining of Debendranath Tagore. His father, Dwarkanath, had been a close associate of Rammohun Roy, and Debendranath had played with Roy's son as a child and had gone to his school. His autobiography relates that he, Debendranath, had venerated Roy early and had followed his example of refraining from participating in Durga Puja.[17] When he was eighteen his grandmother's death had triggered a spiritual crisis which led to Debendranath's joining of the Brahmo Samaj. Despite his friendship with Roy, Dwarkanath opposed his son's spiritual pursuits, but this had the effect of making Debendranath more resolute. Still another opponent, Duff once more, crystallized his thinking with an attack on the Brahmo Samaj in his book, *India and Indian Missions*, in 1845. Duff charged that the Brahmos believed in the infallibility of the Vedas, so Debendranath commissioned a thorough study of the Vedas to clarify their position. The

---

[15]Susobhan Sarkar, *Bengal Renaissance and Other Essays* (New Delhi: People's Publishing House, 1970), p. 122.

[16]*Calcutta Gazette*, December 29, 1831.

[17]*Autobiography of Maharshi Debendranath Tagore*, trans. by Satyendranath Tagore and Indira Devi (London: Macmillan, 1914), pp. 54-57.

conclusion was that the Vedas, Upanishads and other ancient writings were not to be accepted as infallible guides, but that reason and conscience were to be the supreme authority.[18] These same sources, and a preference for a simple theism, surfaced at his father's death in 1846, when Debendranath omitted traditional, but to him idolatrous funeral rites. The directions of the Brahmos for this period were established along devotional paths which depended on ancient Indian theistic, not monistic, sources. His son, Satyendranath, brother of Rabindranath, in his translator's preface to his father's *Autobiography*, observed that he was never known to quote the Hebrew Bible or to refer to Christ in any of his sermons.[19] Perheps he felt that Rammohun Roy's skirmishes with Christianity had been unprofitable; he at least confined his stated sources to those from within the Hindu tradition. In his example the warm devotional wellsprings of Rammohun Roy were renewed in the Brahmo Samaj, along with an awakened appreciation for the ancient religious and cultural wealth of India.

Social reform interests did not, however, thrive under the leadership of Debendranath Tagore. Here the chief mantle passed in this period to Pandit Iswarchandra Vidyasagar, Bengali educator and champion of women's rights. More than any other Indian, perhaps, Vidyasagar relied on the Utilitarian principle of reason. The extent of this reliance is conveyed in a passage by a recent interpreter of Vidyasagar, Amales Tripathi :

His vast knowledge of Hindu shastras taught him of the infinite interpretations to which subjects like God, soul, and rebirth lent themselves. He could never find any one of them logically acceptable as well as conforming to the reality of the human condition. . . .He was not prepared to believe in a kind or merciful God. Akshoykumar Dutt talked of Providence. Vidyasagar scoffed at such an idea, when God (if at all) could allow the sinking of Sir John Lawrence (a steamer) with hundreds of passengers on board or the devastating famine of 1866 which carried off thousands of innocent

18Ibid., pp. 4, 5.
19Ibid., p. 13.

people of Lower Bengal and Orissa. Such a God was irrele-
vant in his virile scheme in which man rescued himself, if he
could, from the buffets of a blind fate. . . .If he had any
religion, it was the religion of humanity, more akin to that of
Comte and Mill than that of the firmly theistic Gita.[20]

Thus, although he was close to a number of the Brahmos, he
did not join them. His career as a reformer was coexistent with
his role as an educator, taking prominent shape when he became General Secretary of a women's school founded in
Calcutta in 1849 by J.E.D. Bethune. With Bethune's death two
years later, Vidyasagar, receiving financial support from notables
such as Lady Dalhousie, continued and began to expand this
work to other locations. R.C. Majumdar credits the founding
and expansion of Bethune's school as "the most important
landmark in the history of women's higher education in
Bengal.[21]

Education was clearly a primary vehicle for women's achievement of their full measure of human dignity in India. As
champion of that cause, Vidyasagar and others saw that the
earlier abolition of *suttee* had saved married women from a
compulsive death, but that more must be done to grant them
the possibility of a fruitful entrance into life.[22] Along with education, then, Vidyasagar worked tirelessly in other areas of
women's rights such as raising the age of marriage, widow's remarriage, rights of widows to inherit, etc. Much of the strategy
for change, obviously, came from raising the level of public
consciousness, but reform through legislation was essential as
well, considering the previously cited rule of custom of which
Vidyasagar was so conscious.

Since the time of the *suttee* legislation the British mood had

[20]Amales Tripathi, *Vidyasagar; the Traditional Modernizer* (Bombay:
Orient Longmans, 1974), pp. 91, 92.

[21]R.C. Majumdar, ed., *The British Paramountcy and Indian Renaissance*, vol. 2, (Bombay: Bhartiya Vidya Bhavan), p. 291.

[22]Arvind Sharma has written a useful article, "Suttee: A study in
Western Reactions," *Journal of Indian History*, December, 1976. In it
he cites Mrs. Marcus B. Fuller, *The Wrongs of Indian Womanhood*
(New York: Young People's Missionary Movement, 1900), in her use
of the term 'cold suttee' referring to the suffering of widows within
Hinduism after the abolition of the act itself.

been one of willingness to act in the sphere of social reform.
H.H. Wilson, noted Orientalist, had written to Bentinck in 1828
against direct action, saying *"Suttee* cannot be put down without interference with the Hindu religion. . . .The attempt, whilst
it will be attended with but partial success, will, in my opinion,
inspire extensive dissatisfaction, and distrust, will alienate, in a
great degree, the affections of the native from their rulers, and
will seriously retard the progress of those better feelings and
sounder notions which are silently but permanently gaining
ground upon the prejudices and practices of the Hindus"[23]
Having determined, however, to intervene, Bentinck and subsequent rulers were reassured by responses such as that in the
Calcutta Gazette shortly after the custom had been abolished:
"The British Government in India has uniformly and satisfactorily demonstrated to the Hindoos the most liberal toleration
of their religion and custom. . . .Toleration has certain impass-
able limits, beyond which lie licentiousness and crime. . . .let
that line be passed, and toleration becomes cruel injustice."[24]
When the feared alienation of the subjects did not follow this
first significant intervention, Britain became less cautious about
successive forceful measures, chiefly in the area of education
and women's rights.

D. In the Aftermath of the Mutiny of 1857

Many reasons have been advanced and interpretations volumi-
nously detailed concerning the causes of the Great Indian Mutiny.
Sir John Kaye early saw it in the light of a Brahmanical protest
against various intrusive measures, others as the first battle for
Indian independence, others as a military rebellion or an
accumulation of private grievances, still others as a combination
of social forces, or a conspiracy, either devised internally or
fomented by Russia.[25] In their response to it, however, the
British seem most to have been influenced by interpretations
which saw the Mutiny as a general protest against interference

[23]Jatindra Kumar Majumdar, ed., *Raja Rammohun Roy and Progressive Movements in India, A Selection From Records, 1775-1845.*
[24]*Calcutta Gazette,* December 7, 1829.
[25]Ainslee T. Embree, ed., *1857 in India: Mutiny or War of Independence?* (Boston: D.C. Heath and Company, 1963), passim.

with established rules and customs. Authority was transferred from the long beleaguered East India Company to direct rule of the Crown in the following year, 1858, but over the balance of the century other policy changes became apparent which were more subtle, but of far-reaching consequence. Benjamin Disraeli's counsel in a speech in the House of Commons just two months after the outbreak of violence seems to have set the tone for a lower profile for Britain in initiating reforms. For Disraeli, native discontent had stemmed from "first, our forcible destruction of native authority; next, our disturbance of the settlement of property; and thirdly, our tempering with the religion of the people."[26] If this was, indeed, an accurate assessment, then a less intrusive presence was called for by Britain. What resulted, then, was that, although visible authority was transferred from Company to Crown, chief responsibility for the initiation of social change was conveyed from the government to the governed. A few isolated leaders had emerged before this pivotal date from among the people. After this with a more timid power center, the public itself must generate incentives for change. The British were fearful of creating further rebellious conditions. In their hesitancy, they seem instead to have produced a power vacuum soon to be filled with political, cultural and religious enthusiasts.

[26]Ibid., pp. 4-12.

| Direction of Reforms and Renewal
Throughout India, 1858-1900

A. NEW ASSESSMENTS

Insofar as the reasons for the Mutiny seemed primarily military
and political in character, different persons offered policy
changes in the direction of a more forceful military presence.
Dalhousie, Governor-General from 1848-1856, was one of the
ablest of British administrators in the nineteenth century, a
convinced westernizer and promoter of public works. Taken to
task for not foreseeing the Mutiny, he acknowledged this failure
but asked, "Who did?" Militarily he claimed to have augmented
the European infantry by 37% since 1848, and that it would have
been over 50% if he had had his way. He felt, also, that Oude
should have been disarmed after annexation, as was the Punjab in
1849, perhaps stemming the tide of insurrection which originated
there.[1] As Spear has noted, "Public works rather than public
morals or western values was the guiding star of the post-mutiny
reformer,"[2] so some of Dalhousie's guidelines may have perse-
vered. The Westernization seems to have been, again, not so
much in the direction of intrusion into the workings of society
subsequently, but a tighter hold on the reins of governance.
During the Mutiny, *The Westminster Review* published an article
which expressed his forceful view:

> We have introduced our super-refined notions of law and jus-
> tice among a people the most corrupt of all semi-barbarians.

[1] G.J.A. Baird, *Private Letters of the Marquess of Dalhousie* (Edin-
burgh: Wm. Blackwood and Sons, 1910), pp. 408, 409, 399.
[2] Percival Spear, *A History of India,* vol. 2 (Baltimore: Penguin
Books, 1965), p. 144.

We have been delicate where we should have been rough, and
lenient where we should have been rigorous. . . . Of all the
absurd things which have been said or done for India, there
is none more absurd than the cry which demands a share of
the government for the natives. . . We have won the country by virtue of our superiority, and we must retain it on the
same theory. . . . To talk of representative institutions for
India is mere drivelling. No country was ever more unfit for
a representative system. . . . In India, the theory of Government
is, and must be, simple despotism. The only choice for us is
between a despotism of brute force, and one of reason and
justice.[3]

The arrogance of this position, obviously, does not allow for
reform, or anticipate a gradual policy of relinquishing of rule.
As the mandate was transferred from the Company to the Crown
in 1858, there was, however, a new sensitivity to Indian public
opinion. This gave at least the educated classes a sounding
board with the British, who did not care for further surprises
after the Mutiny. But the pulse on the native mind could not be
so privately used to solidify the British *raj*. Indian leaders began
to emerge; they were articulate. They began to consolidate
into movements, agitating, prodding the reluctant British dragon.
The history of the balance of the century is the record of such
increasingly insistent initiatives.

B. IN BENGAL

Reform interests in the Brahmo Samaj had languished under
the leadership of Debendranath Tagore, but these began again
to surface when the zealous Keshab Chander Sen joined the
group in 1857 at the age of nineteen. At his behest, Tagore yielded the wearing of the red thread to mark the upper castes in
Brahmo gatherings, but when, after the meeting place of the
Samaj burned in 1860 and sessions were held in his own home,
Debendranath once more allowed the practice. For Keshab,
Brahmoism was catholic and universal, not equivalent with

---

[3]John Chapman, "The English in India, "*Westminster Review*,
January 1858, pp. 204-208.

Hinduism. Caste distinctions compromised this universality. His own positive act of marrying two persons of different castes in 1863 further widened his difference with Tagore, and a split in the Samaj followed. Keshab's group was known formally as the Brahmo Samaj of India, or more popularity as The New Dispensation, with Debendranath's group being known henceforth as The Adi (or original) Brahmo Samaj.

Politically, Keshab was not anti-British in temper, rather proclaiming loyalty to the British as an article and creed of his Church. This was further intensified through his six-month visit to the West in 1870. Nationalism, thus, was incorporated for Keshab with wider affiliative ties, but this universalistic spirit was not without its appeal. His own oratorical gifts and personal magnetism in his tours of India did in fact give his movement something of an all-India status. He had an almost evangelical fervor in the proclamation of his message, and began soon to send out other missionaries as well. One custom, for which Ramakrishna would later chide the Brahmos, called the Festival of Rejoicing in the Lord, seems particularly Western in character. Begun by Keshab in 1867, the festival was spoken of by his biographer, Miss Collet, as follows: "Now for the first time in connection with the Brahmo Samaj was witnessed the rare spectacle of sinful men, bitterly conscious of their sins, praying and listening with living sincerity for their soul's salvation."[4]

In addition, then, to learning from the West in content and style of worship, Keshab felt free to cooperate with British rulers in initiating reform measures. At his urging the British passed the Native Marriage Act in 1872, authorizing unorthodox marriages between persons declaring themselves neither Hindu, Muslim or Christian. It also made monogamy obligatory and fixed minimum ages at 18 and 14 for the groom and bride taking advantage of it. A new schism in the Samaj developed, however, just six years later, when Keshab allowed his daughter to be married to the Prince of Cooch Behar although both were under the ages specified in the above Act. Keshab had developed Debendranath's doctrine of intuition to

---

[4]Nemai Sadhan Bose, *The Indian Awakening and Bengal* (Calcutta: Firma K.L. Mukhopadhyay, 1960), p. 97.

the point that he was almost a law unto himself. The resultant movement appears to have become an almost classic charismatic organization,[5] with few guidelines, depending on the often vacillating directions taken by the leader. In this case, his defenders, convinced of their leader's integrity, felt that he could not go against the express guidance which he claimed to have received,[6] but this did not satisfy those in the movement who demanded a more consistent policy of reform. The Sadharan Brahmo Samaj was thus formed, breaking away from the New Dispensation, and having in general a more rationalistic and less theistic temper.

The influence of the Brahmos in general was to wane by the end of the century. They had generated, with varying intensity, considerable support for social change, and in patterns of worship, their freedom to incorporate materials from many traditions was liberating for some. But the circle of influence remained limited to the *bhadralok*, the cultural elite, for the most part. The New Dispensation and the Sadharan Brahmo Samaj seemed too westernized in their borrowings, cut-flower bouquets which had lost their rootage in the Indian tradition. And the Adi Brahmo Samaj began to be restricted more and more to the activities of the Tagore family circle, having moved closer to orthodox Hinduism and losing much of its character as a reform movement.

Again, however, not all indigenous religious change in Bengal emanated from the Brahmos. The Ramakrishna Movement will be discussed in detail in the next chapter, and the activities of two other Bengalis should here be mentioned. One, Bankimchandra Chatterji, was born the same year as Keshab and attended Presidency College in Calcutta at the same time. His early professional activities were in journalism. In 1872 he began to publish the journal *Bangadarsan* which, in the judgment of one historian, "soon became the ablest and most

[5]Max Weber, *The Sociology of Religion* (Boston: Beacon Press, 1963), pp. 46, 47.
[6]Gouri Prasad Mazoomdar, *Keshub Chander Sen and the Schools of Protest and Non-Protest* (Calcutta: The Art Press, n.d.), pp. 49-54. See also Dwijadas Datta, *Behold the Man* (Calcutta: Dwijadas Dutta, 1930), pp. 135-140.

influential monthly magazine in Bengal."[7] Rabindranath Tagore wrote of it: *"Then came Bankim's Bangadarsan,* taking the Bengali heart by storm. It was bad enough to have to wait until the next monthly number was out, but to be kept waiting further till my elders had done with it was simply intolerable."[8] Bankim attempted, also, to reach the masses with the publication of a moral biography of Krishna. While his historical methodology seems dubious to the Indian scholar R. C. Majumdar, he provided a strong defense against missionary attacks on Krishna's character.[9] Religious renewal was linked with nationalism for him, also, so that worshipping India became underlying theme of devotion to the various goddesses. His writings, such as *Anand Math,* voiced this, as did his stirring poem, *Bande Mataram,* which was to become the national anthem for India.

But Bankim was not an uncritical patriot. He had harsh language for his own caste, the Kulin Brahmins, in his second novel, and for Tantrism, which seemed extremely debased to him.[10] Both the sensual and spiritual solutions were wrong in his thought, because each could avoid the *karma* component which he saw as central, following instead the indulgent or ascetic path. He saw the *sannyasi,* or monastic, as being often a shirker of duty. Bengalis as a whole came under his sarcastic wit at times as when he spoke of them as a "class of people who had learned craftiness from the fox, sycophancy and love of begging from the dog, cowardice from the sheep, imitativeness from the monkey and noisiness from the ass."[11] Despite these invectives against his own, Bankim conveyed an idealistic vision to his countrymen based on traditional values.

The militancy of Surendranath (often altered to Surrender-not, with some accuracy) Banerjee cannot be explained by his early personal contacts with the British, which were, by his own account, benign. He states, "My Anglo-Indian and European teachers and professors were throughout very kind to me, and

[7]Jayanta Kumar Das Gupta, *A Critical Study of the Life and Novels of Bankimchandra* (Calcutta: Calcutta University, 1937), p. 22.
[8]Ibid., p. 24.
[9]Majumdar, op. cit., p. 116.
[10]Das Gupta, op. cit., p. 25.
[11]Ibid., pp. 147, 148.

they did not show a particle of racial feeling in their treatment
of me. In that temple of learning, in which I passed some of
my happiest years, I was never allowed to hear the faintest echo
of those racial and sectarian controversies that sometimes dis-
tracted the country."[12] His father, a doctor, had had a liberal education at Hindu College under David Hare. He provided that
his son, Surendranath, should also have an English education,
and he was in fact among the first Indians to complete this in
England. Through apparently biased and prejudicial machina-
tions, however, he was dismissed from Indian Civil Service
after a short time and also refused admittance to the Bar after
further preparation in London. From these experiences he
began to identify with the powerless in his homeland. Thus his
professional career as an educator was augmented consistently
by political activity. Beginning under Vidyasagar as a professor
of English, he then taught at City College in 1879, just after it
was opened by the Sadharan Brahmo Samaj. Vivekanand, whom
we shall meet in the next chapter, was regularly in his lectures
during this period. In 1882 Banerjee took charge of Presidency
College, remaining primarily an educator till 1912, when he was
elected to the Imperial Legislature Council in Delhi.

In 1876 he began the Indian Association for land reform,
and four additional objectives: 1) the creation of a strong body
of public opinion; 2) the unification of the Indian races and
people on the basis of common political interests and aspirations;
3) the promotion of friendly feeling between Hindus and
Mohammedans and 4) the inclusion of the masses in the great
public movements of the day. He took over the publication of
The *Bengalee*, an influential journal, to further advance these
goals.[13]

C. In Western India

The Prarthana Samaj in the west grew out of Keshab's missionary activities, but from its inception it seemed to exhibit less
of a spirit of adolescent rebellion than the parent organization,

---

[12]Surendranath Banerjee, *A Nation in Making* (Bombay: Oxford
University Press, 1963), p. 3.
[13]Ibid., pp. 39, 62.

with perhaps less, also, of the characteristic Bengali emotional volatility. In this it mirrored the more judicious and moderate tone generally in the Bombay Presidency. Reform was less root and branch than in Bengal, with greater concern to preserve historic ties to the ancestral faith. Thus there was nothing equivalent to the Brahmo Marriage Bill, which in Bengal had in effect created a separate caste or religion. A greater feeling for national, as against regional issues was also to emerge through the activities of men such as Ranade, Tilak and Gokhale, the latter to emerge as Ranade's successor by the century's end.

Ranade and Tilak, the early leaders, differed markedly in their strategies and goals. Ranade's efforts were comprehensive, embracing political organization and social and religious reform. Tilak directed none of his energies to social reform, but his political objectives were more radical than those of Justice Ranade, and were linked closely, also, to his religious ideas. Ranade founded both the Indian National Congress and the Social Conference, which he hoped might further political and reform interests, prospering together. From the time the Social Congress began in 1887 its sessions were in fact held with those of the National Congress till into the 1900s.

As a member of the Prarthana Samaj, Ranade was theistic, believing in the moral government of a perfect being and the immortality of the soul as the purest form of religion, and indeed, as the crown of India's religious development.[14] He drew a parallel between the medieval poet saints of India and Protestant reformers in Europe, coining the name Hindu Protestantism for his reform efforts. The loving god which he found in these two historical strains could not sanction Brahmanism, with its trappings of Sanskrit supremacy, rites and ceremonies, Yoga austerities and powers, caste rules and distinctions, animal and human sacrifices, the worship of cruel deities, shakta rites and polytheism.[15] His appeal was not only to the ancient texts, but to the age of the Grihya Sutras as exemplary, in

---

[14]M.G. Ranade, *Religious and Social Reform, a Collection of Essays and Speeches* (Bombay: Gopal Narayan and Co., 1902), passim.

[15]Ibid., p. 200. See also M.G. Ranade, *The Rise of Maratha Power* (Bombay: Punalikar and Co., 1900), chapter 8.

which women, for instance, assumed leadership roles beside those of male pandits and philosophers.[16]

Specifics on religion and nationalism will be deferred, but the fascinating reasons behind Tilak's contrasting position should here be delineated in brief. He opposed the social reformers on two counts, both of which had some credibility. First, he felt that the reformers did not consistently practice the new life style which they sought to impose on the larger society. Tilak's personal example did in fact appear more modern often than that of certain reformers. He opposed governmental interference, though he was committed to going beyond the age limitations then being proposed for marriage legislation. He was one of the first five signators on a pledge in 1889 to educate his daughters and not marry them before the age of ten, and did not actually marry them till they were over sixteen.[17] Tilak's second objection was his feeling that activities in social reform were an admission of weakness. To alleviate the shortcomings of society, the reformers were both imitating the European overlords and cooperating with them to effect change in a way which would solidify their rule. His watchword was, "Swaraj is my birthright and I will have it," and this dictated a policy of non-cooperation. He thus opposed the Age of Consent Bill, ultimately passed by the Viceroy's Legislative Council in 1891, because the social reformers were modifying Indian Society and the Hindu religion by use of British law. Rigorously anti-Western, Tilak felt that this amounted to hand-in-glove collaboration.

For Ranade, the work of providence itself was seen in the moral ends which the coming of the British served, such as the widening of the ideals of social justice and extension of human rights generally. The issue was not whether these ideas originated in India or anywhere else; they were needed at present in India. "India is indeed fortunate, " Ranade observed, " in that the knowledge she should seek from the British is close at hand.

[16]M.G. Ranade, *Miscellaneous Writings* (Bombay: Manoranjan Press, 1915), pp. 71-74.

[17]S. Natarajan, *A Century of Social Reform in India* (New York: Asia Publishing House, 1959), p. 66. See also Charles Heimsath, *Indian Nationalism and Hindu Social Reform* (Princeton: Princeton University Press, 1964), p. 209.

Instead of decrying the impact upon India of western thought the true lover of India will rejoice in it."[18]

But if Ranade and others seemed too temperate in political reform for Tilak, the middle path of each made them equally vulnerable to attack from genuinely radical social reformers. When Ranade and Tilak, both Chitpavan Brahmins, submitted to caste demands that they publicly repent for having taken food at a tea party given by Christian missionaries, it was a moment of sharp disillusionment for many. *The Social Reformer*, published first from Madras in 1890 and later in Bombay, had harsh criticism for what it regarded as personal vacillation and public timidity. As an English language periodical, committed to rationalistic rather than Scriptural bases for reform, the *Reformer* largely ignored the conventions to which the earlier reformers in western India continued to feel amenable.

As the century turned, then, the movement was fired with a greater fervency. The causes of female education, widow's rights, and greater maturity before marital consummation still had gains to make, but the younger reformers wanted to break new ground. Their causes, unlike the earlier ones, would threaten the caste structure itself. Among these would be the active promotion of intercaste dining—the issue from which Ranade and Tilak retreated—and the first stirrings of conscience about the plight of the untouchable.[19]

Western India also produced one of the singular woman reformers of the nineteenth century, Pandita Ramabai. Born, like Tilak, Ranade and Gokhale into the Chitpavan Brahmin caste,

[18]James Kellock, *Mahadev Govind Ranade, Patriot and Social Servant* (Calcutta: Association Press, 1926), p. 13.

[19]Dr. B.R. Ambedkar, twentieth century reformer and primary drafter of the Indian Constitution, himself an untouchable, credits Mahatma Phule with starting the first school for untouchables in India, in 1852 in Poona. Ambedkar's book, *Who Were the Shudras?* was dedicated as follows: "Inscribed to the memory of Mahatma Jyotiba Phule, 1827-1890, the greatest Shundra of Modern India, who made the lower classes of Hindus conscious of their slavery to the higher classes and who preached the gospel that for India, social democracy was more vital than independence from foreign rule." Quoted in G.S Lokhande, *Bhimrao Ramji Ambedkar* (New Delhi: Sterling Publishers Ltd., 1977), p. 9. See also Dhananjay Keer, *Dr. Ambedkar, Life and Mission* (Bombay: Popular Prakashan 1962), p. 4.

she had the early advantage of traveling widely, since her father was an itinerant Puranic scholar. In her wanderings with her parents, she saw the current status of women, their subjection to men, their lack of education. She became a recognized Sanskrit and Puranic scholar in her own right, thus earning the appelation Pandita. She married out of her caste in Bengal, and when her husband died of cholera after a year and a half, she was left destitute with an infant daughter.

The Pandita came to Poona, the center of reform in western India, in 1882 to work for women's education. Her fame as a scholar and lecturer had preceded her, but her marriage and her ideas on education caused opposition from Brahmins. She started an organization for women's rights but, disappointed with the response, she began to seek support elsewhere. Encouraged by missionaries, she traveled to England, where she openly became a Christian. In England and the United States she toured to gain financial backing for the home she planned for widows . A part of her indictment against the treatment of women in India was contained in her book, *High Caste Hindu Women*. Various Ramabai Associations were formed in the West to help her with her work.

Upon returning to India in 1889, the Pandita began the Sarada Sadan for widows. Replying to criticism of her having become a Christian, she censured her opponents in return for their dog-in-the-manger attitude, saying that it was because she could not get help from Hindus that she went to Christians. The Sarada Sadan was soon avowedly Christian. The Indian historian D. S. Sarma has said of her, "Like Mrs. Besant, (she was) one of those rare souls who, born in one religion and driven by their past Karma into another, feel instinctively at home there and find in it perfect satisfaction for all their spiritual needs as well as full scope for their ambitious personalities."[20]

D. IN SOUTHERN INDIA

The pace of reform in the south of India was generally slower than elsewhere, although in at least two respects reform was

[20]D.S. Sarma, *Studies in the Renaissance of Hinduism* (Benares: Benares Hindu University, 1944), p. 134.

less needed. English language study had by the latter part of the century been more widespread here than elsewhere in India. At the same time, however, only a small percentage of students went on to imbibe the university climate which, in Bengal, produced so much of the ferment for reform. But in the area of land reform, the situation was clearly much better than in Bengal. There the British had reinforced the unique *zamindari* system, in which the peasant, being landless, was also largely voiceless. In the Madras Presidency, however, the *ryotwar* (small farm) system was operative, with less social distance between the peasant and the elite.

Brahmins, however, were still dominant in the Madras Presidency, and reform activities were restricted mostly to puritanical concerns such as the elimination of *nautch* dancing in connection with the temples and the prohibition of beverage alcohol. In its short career in Madras before moving to Bombay, *The Social Reformer* had served to awaken the conscience of South Indians on larger issues, but prior to that a heroic figure, Viresalingam, was an almost solitary voice. He could be, in the breadth of his concerns, at one moment a critic of British rule, at another pressing for widow remarriage.

Reform was also intimidated in the south by the presence of the Theosophical Society after 1882. The Society became the bulwark of the established social order for many years so that, even though orthodox Hindus might not actively relate to it, they relied on it to defend the traditional positions against the onslaughts of the reformers. That Westerners were championing orthodox social practice was a great conservative counteragency to social change.

The history of Theosophy in nineteenth century India is replete with colorful personalities, schisms arising between them and other movements, periodic scandals, and occult teachings which augmented those of the native faiths. Colonel Olcott and Madame Blavatsky had established the Society in New York City in 1875. Substantial activity began with the publication by Madame Blavatsky of her first book, *Isis Unveiled*, and initiation of correspondence with Swami Dayananda Saraswati of the Arya Samaj of India. In obedience to the leadings of the Tibetan Masters, who were throughout the movement's early history credited as a primary source of mystical direction, Blavatsky and Olcott came to India in 1879. There they landed in Bombay to a welcome from Dayananda and his followers in the Arya Samaj. The Western pair's early efforts paralleled those of the Arya Samaj in reforming education, promoting Sanskrit learning, and generally seeking to counter the influence of Christian missionaries. The association with the Samaj lasted only a year, but it was useful in getting a foothold for Theosophy.

During that year, Blavatsky records her high opinion of Dayananda in an aside in one of her voluminous scrapbooks. An article is clipped from an unknown source, undated precisely, which records the response of a Dr. Husband, medical missionary at Ajmere, to Swami Dayananda. Husband's own assessment of his encounter with Dayananda was positive, and he stated, "We felt a solemn and bounden duty rested on us to show them (orthodox Hindus) and others that the Pandit's objections could be satisfactorily answered, and with God's blessing, to lead them to a purer faith and nobler worship." Blavatsky's hand note, in a column beneath, says, "Vain hope! my Reverend, Better and abler scholars than you came out 'second best' with Swami."[21]

Blavatsky and Olcott themselves made a fascinating team, the former having a vague and mysterious past including the disputed claim of having spent years in Tibet. This added to her aura as foundress of what became the esoteric branch of the society. Much could be written of her research into the occult and the ways in which she was reputed to have established contact with her arcane sources. Olcott later reported, "She often said to me that her true existence only began when nightly she had put her body to sleep and went out of it to the Masters."[22] The contrast, accordingly, was also expressed by Olcott : "We each had our department of work—hers the mystical, mine the practical."[23] And Olcott was eminently fitted for his role, also. He had held important positions with the Department of Agriculture, the War and Navy Departments

---

[21]H.P. Blavatsky, *Scrapbook*, 1879, p. 7. Courtesy, The Archives of the Theosophical Society, Adyar,

[22]Colonel Henry Steel Olcott, editorial in *Theosophist*, July, 1891, p. 577.

[23]Ibid.

during the Civil War, and as a lawyer had acted as Commissioner "for the investigation of frauds upon the Government in the purchase of Army supplies."[24] After the war, he was in private practice for several years and then was Secretary of the National Insurance Convention of the United States. In going to India he was given a special diplomatic passport and a letter of recommendation by President Rutherford B. Hayes to United States Ministers and Consuls, stating that he would "make reports from time to time regarding the condition and prospects of commerce between the United States and India."[25]

Olcott's diplomatic qualities surfaced many times, as when he wrote concerning Dayananda after the Theosophical Society and Arya Samaj had parted company :

"The opponents of Pandit Dayananda Saraswati Swami may as well understand at the outset, that the columns of the "Theosophist" are not open to indiscriminate attacks upon him or the Arya Samaj. Because there is a rupture of the relations of our Society with him, it is no reason why we should make our paper the channel for the ventilation (of hostilities). We have kept silence as to our own grievances, and we do not feel bound to take up the quarrels of others . . . . The question of the Swami's Vedic scholarship is one that may be left for the Pandits of India and Europe to decide; and, however much we may grieve to see so learned a man carried away by such wild misconceptions in our case, no one can deny that he is a loyal champion of Aryan culture, and imbued with a patriot's feeling for his native land. That he should be true to our alliance is of far less consequence, than that he should be true to India."[26]

The first journal of the Society, *The Theosophist*, began publication from Bombay in October of 1879, defining itself as "A Monthly Journal Devoted to Oriental Philosophy, Art, Literature, and Occultism; Embracing Mesmerism, Spiritualism,

[24]Quotation from the *Simla Courier*, August 26, 1881 in *Amrita Bazar Patrika*, April 1, 1880.
[25]Ibid.
[26]H.S. Olcott, editorial in *Theosophist*, May, 1872.

and Other Secret Sciences."[27] It traced the origins of Theosophy to Ammonius Saccas, founder of Neo-Platonists, but with other Alexandrian and also the Orphic Mysteries, which, it claimed, originated in India. "Theosophy is, then, the archaic Wisdom-Religion, the esoteric doctrine once known in every ancient country having claims to civilization."[28] It stated that it held no belief structure as a body, that it had no creed, that it was, in fact, no more sectarian than a geographical society. Another journal, The Indian Spectator, which had been responsible on the Indian scene for some time, greeted the apppearance of the Theosophist and its premises with a humorously satirical editorial: "He (The Theosophist) is a promising youth and does infinite credit to his parents. His nurses, too, wet and dry, have to be congratulated." Dry nurses cited in the editorial are the recognized Indian philosophical sources and wet ones are esoteric ones of doubtful referrent, such as, "The Swami of Akalkot (Dayananda?), The Dead Devil, The Ensouled Violin, etc." This fare, it suggests, may "be too heavy for the Theosophist digestion, . . . as if turning sour . . . We are tremendously anxious that Theosophist should not become an enfant terrible and thus horrify the authors of its being." The editorial departs from its whimsical note to critique the journal for its too hasty attack on Christian missions, however.[29]

After its break with the Arya Samaj, Olcott and Blavatsky moved in 1880 to Ceylon, feeling an affinity with Buddhism and wishing to lend support there against missionary initiatives. Among the important contacts made in Ceylon were one with a Buddhist youth later to be known as Dharmapala, founder of the Mahabodhi Society. Theosophy did not locate long in Ceylon, however, but made its headquarters on an estate at Adyar, just south of Madras. where it has remained till the present day. Back in India, it sought to stimulate a new pride in the country, its traditions and customs. Amrita Bazar Patrika recorded the testimony of one high British official, who said, from his contacts with Theosophy, "I am astounded when I see how all my feelings towards the Natives have changed within

---

[27]Theosophist, vol. 1, p. no. 11, October, 1879.
[28]Ibid., pp. 2, 3.
[29]Editorial in The Indian Spectator, January 18, 1880, p. 30.

the past year."[30] A. O. Hume, who assisted in the founding of the Indian National Congress, was related to Theosophy also, and the *Simla Courier* lists him as President of the Simla Eclectic Theosophical Society in 1881.[31]

Despite such associations and achievements, Madame Blavatsky left India under something of a cloud several years after locating in Adyar. An investigation of the Society's claim of letters from the Tibetan Masters had been pressed by the Society for Psychical Research in London, and their report, later disputed, indicted Madame Blavatsky as a fraud and the Society's claim to have received occult phenomena as spurious. Blavatsky then settled in London where she died in 1891. Olcott's tribute to her in the *Theosophist* confessed that, "Despite seventeen years of intimacy in daily work, she was an enigma to me to the end."[32] Even for her close associate and friend, the mystery remained, but his words also mirror the lingering controversy which had dogged her career. "Her life, as I have known it these past seventeen years, has been a tragedy, the tragedy of a martyr-philanthropist. Burning with zeal for the spiritual welfare and intellectual enfranchisement of humanity, moved by no selfish inspiration, given herself freely and without price to her altruistic work, she has been hounded to her death-day, by the slanderer, the bigot, and the Pharisee . . . . For pity's sake, let the dead lioness lie in peace, and seek a more ignoble carcase upon which to vomit."[33]

If the closing years were marred for Blavatsky with rumor and scandal, she gained a disciple in London who was to be profoundly useful in the Society's subsequent history. Annie Besant was already a public figure in Victorian England, having separated from her husband to become a leader in free thought and socialism. Blavatsky's mantle was sharply disputed, with W. Q. Judge, an officer of the Society from its inception in 1875, producing two letters supposedly from one of Blavatsky's mystic sources, which supported his claim as Blavatsky's rightful heir. Leaders of the Society initially yielded to this claim,

[30]*Amrita Bazar Patrika*, op. cit.
[31]Ibid.
[32]Olcott, *Theosophist*, July, 1891, p. 574.
[33]Ibid.

but when the letters were deemed fraudulent a split in the Society occured, with Judge leading most American Theosophists into a separate movement. This was called The Universal Brotherhood and Theosophical Society, and its members elected Judge their President for Life. He lived, however, only eleven months longer. For the parent Society in Adyar, however, much of the primary authority passed to Annie Besant, who with a few others represented Theosophy in the 1893 Parliament of Religions in Chicago, and then took passage to India. She developed a deep feeling for her adopted country, which she regarded as having been the place of her birth in a previous incarnation, and swiftly set about to instill a new vitality in Hinduism. In addition to Olcott, who remained with her a revered leader, C. W. Leadbetter, formerly a curate of the Church of England, became one of the Society's ranking officials at about this time. His subsequent contributions were most significant in the esoteric branch of Theosophy.

Shortly after arriving in India, Mrs. Besant stated publicly, "My work in the sphere of politics is over, and I shall never resume it."[34] For over twenty years she maintained considerable fidelity to that declaration, being wholly identified with the revival of Hinduism and not at all with reform. But this early career as a revivalist was by no means solely negative in character. Through her efforts, for instance, the Sanskrit tradition received a vital transfusion, and her most noted contribution to the Indian scene at large may lie in the field of education. This would be strikingly apparent later in the great part she played in the founding of Benares Hindu University, but also in the many schools she began for both girls and boys. The Society can claim other educational initiatives from the nineteenth century, among them the schools which Olcott began for untouchable boys beginning in 1894. Thus, while the movement's activities were in the direction largely of defense of the traditional societal structures, it was not blind to India's problems.

E. In Northern India

The Arya Samaj, previously mentioned in connection with

---

[34]Supplement to *Theosophist*, March, 1894,

Theosophy, belongs largely to northern India. The founder, Dayananda, like his junior by a few years, Ramakrishna, had little exposure to Western influence. Unlike Ramakrishna, however, he was learned in Sanskrit, and the reforms which he advocated were based on his study of Vedas and certain teachings from the Code of Manu. He sought to restore a purer Hinduism after a Vedic model, for he believed that Puranic distortions had weakened Hinduism with idolatry and other corrupt influences. In temperament he exhibited nothing of the warm *bhakti* (devotional) strain that we shall witness in Ramakrishna.

The deaths of a sister and an uncle appear to have deepened his already serious nature, and he resisted his parents' efforts to stabilize him in a householder state by changing his name and leaving home to become a *sadhu* (ascetic mendicant) on the day designated for his wedding. Fifteen years of wandering, during which he practiced yoga and became immersed in Vedanta philosophy, ended when at long last he was able to find a guru able to instruct him deeply in Vedic lore. The blind teacher Virajananda was a severe taskmaster, often applying physical discipline and, before the instruction could even begin, required Dayananda to throw his modern books into the Jamuna River as a symbol of cutting himself off from all that was recent in scholarship. But Virajananda was a master of Sanskrit grammar, and the disciple stayed with him for two and a half years, perfecting his knowledge of the earliest and most authoritative literature of his people. Then Dayananda began to wander about, preaching against idolatry and debating with scholars about the essential teachings of Hinduism. His travels eventually took him to Calcutta, where he encountered Keshab Chandra Sen and other Brahmo leaders and Ramakrishna. The latter shared his impressions of Dayananda to his disciples, as follows: "I went to see him in the garden of Sinthi: I found that he had acquired a little power; his chest was always red . . . . He misapplied grammer and twisted the meaning of many words. He had in his mind the egoism, I'll do something, I'll found a doctrine.' "[35] Dayananda resisted the Westernization of the Brahmos, and did not know English,

[35]Swami Saradananda, *Sri Ramakrishna, The Great Mastar* (Madras: Sri Ramakrishna Math, 1952), p. 551.

but he apparently followed Keshab's suggestion that he carry on his teaching in the vernacular rather than Sanskrit to reach the people with his message. B. C. Pal credits him with being able powerfully to reach the emotions of the masses in a way that the Brahmos never tried. The Brahmos, however, admired Dayananda's enlightened views on the caste structure and on idol worship, although his opposition to the latter was decidedly more emphatic than that of the Brahmos. Other Vedic ordinances on which he insisted, also in contrast to the Brahmos, were veneration of the cow and the daily butter sacrifice on the hearth fire.[36]

Dayananda moved from Calcutta to Bombay, where he formally founded the Arya Samaj in 1875. The relationship with the Theosophical Society was soon initiated, but there were inevitable differences. One might suspect that the occult elements in Theosophy would have repelled Dayananda, as we know that his strong polemic against Christianity and Islam was not acceptable to those in Theosophy. He wrote Madame Blavatsky, "As night and day are opposed to each other, so are all religions opposed to one another.[37] Accordingly, he inaugurated a strong policy of *suddhi*, or reconversion of those who had become Muslim or Christian. Orthodox Hinduism had strictly opposed such readmission.[38] He aggressively sought to counter the tide of defections from Hinduism, pursuing converts from the ranks of these other faiths as well. Perhaps his residence in the west and north of India, where a history of militant opposition between Hinduism and Islam was strongest, may have influenced him. At any rate, the universalism with which other reformers sought to clothe their understanding of Hinduism was absent to him. His call for classic education has, however, been answered by the movement which continued following his death in 1883, although later Arya Samaj institutions did much more than he would have sanctioned with English education.

Lala Lajpat Rai, who later assumed national stature as a

[36]Majumdar, op. cit., p. 109.

[37]Heimsath, op. cit., p. 122.

[38]For an elaborated discussion of the issues involved in the practice of *shuddhi*, see J.T.F. Jordens, "Reconversion to Hinduism, The Shuddhi of the Arya Samaj," in G.A. Oddie, editor, *Religion in South India* (New Delhi: Manohar Book Service, 1977), pp. 145-161.

leader, was initiated into the Arya Samaj at the age of 17, a year before Dayananda's death. His autobiography records the extravagant tribute which he paid to the Samaj: "All that was evil in me I must have inherited either from those who brought me into being, or from my own previous lives, and all that was good and creditable in me I owed to the Arya Samaj."[39] Pal's appreciation is more qualified. Yet despite the violence which he felt that Dayananda did to the modern rational spirit and the universality of the Vedas, he credits Dayananda with doing more to enhance Hindu pride than did the leaders of the Brahmo Samaj.[40] Arya members themselves maintained the critique of the Brahmos as being too westernized, even Christianized.

"We have held it from the very first that Brahmoism was but a perverted or distorted form of Christianity . . . . Pick up any Brahmo paper, and therein you will find the most unmistakable proofs of the fact that the original source of Brahmoism is the religion of Christ. Christianity constituted, as it were, the vital principle of Brahmoism, it is the source of its life, vigor and strength."[41]

For the Arya Samaj, sometimes referred to as "The Church Militant in Hinduism," the eclecticism of the Brahmos was treasonous to the Tradition.

Another very significant movement from northern India which began in the nineteenth century was the Radhasoami faith. Emerging out of the tradition of late medieval *bhakti* saints, its teachings, as recognized by Farquhar and as acknowledged by Agam Prasad Mathur, writing as a critical

[39]Lala Lajpat Rai, *Young India* (Delhi: Ministry of Information and Broadcasting, (1965), p. 6.

[40]Majumdar, op. cit., pp. 114, 115.

[41]Kenneth W. Jones, *Arya Dharm: Hindu Consciousness in 19th Century Punjab*, (Berkeley: University of California Press, 1976), p. 114. Jones identifies his study, actually the first of three projected volumes, as the history of a process rather than a movement. While it does not, thus, exclusively focus on the Arya Samaj, it does recognize the dominance of that group in the process and is an extremely valuable work.

historian and leader of the movement, are remarkably similar
to those of Theosophy. Mathur states:

"Theosophy, basing its teachings upon oriental beliefs, bears
striking similarities to the Radhasoami faith. Both empha-
size the esoteric mode of religious life. Propagating spiritualism, theosophy not only revived the faith of enlightened
Hindus, but also inadvertently endorsed the mystic revela-
tions stressed by Radhasoamis. The almost identical theories with regard to the economy of creation, laws of karma,
and theory of spiritually enlightened souls, are strikingly
similar between the two mystic faiths. People of every caste,
creed and nationality are admitted into both folds without
the pre-requisite of a change of label. But the method of
spiritual practice recommended in the Radhasoami faith
appears to be more logical and scientific than the one favored
in theosophy. However, the contribution of the Theosophical Society in the field of education is greater than that of
the Radhasoami faith."[42]

The movement had its formal beginnings in 1861 in Agra
with the teachings of Shiv Dayal Singh, who was born in 1818.
His father, a Punjabi Sikh and devotee of Nanak, had settled
in Agra as a banker. Although British educated, the son,
Dayal, was more immersed in the lore and teachings of the
family saint, Nanak, and other devotional poets. Despite the
name given the sect by the second guru, Saligram, who provided much of its organizational structure and direction from
1878—1898, there is little evidence that the founders or followers gave the movement anything of the character of a
Vaishnava devotional sect. Mathur, for instance, disputes
Farquhar's contention that Dayal and his wife ever played ritual
roles of Krishna and Radha.[43] Farquhar does seem accurate, however, in noting that the name itself, Radhasoami (the latter name
is a curious spelling of *swami*), bears four meanings for the sect.

     [42]Agam Prasad Mathur, *Radhasoami Faith*: *A Historical Study*
(Delhi: Vikas Publishing House, 1974), p. 154.
     [43]Ibid., p. 37. See also J.N. Farquhar, *Modern Religious Movements
in India* (Delhi: Munshiram Manoharlal, 1967), 166.

"It is the name of God Himself; it is the name which the first guru bears, as the perfect incarnation of God; it is the name which the spiritual sound-current (Sabda) makes as it rings through all religions; and it is the name of the sect."[44]

The second guru had left government service to assume religious obedience under Dayal, the horrors of the Indian Mutiny having changed the directions of his life goals, according to Max Mueller, who knew him personally.[45] He, Saligram, was able to structure patterns of worship, a sense of community, and a theology sufficiently sophisticated to appeal to persons in contact with modern scientific and philosophical thought. It seeks to transcend many of the trappings such as images and pilgrimages of other devotional cults, to offer direct access to the divine who is made known through a succession of *Santsatgurus*, or manifestations of the Supreme Being on Earth. These master teachers alone have the key to the inner spiritual practice whereby the *surat* (spirit entity) is united with the *shabad* (the holy resonance of the sound current).[46] One relates to one's own teacher within, the tradition, then, as the one who can reflect what the master teacher of the time imparts of the Divine.

With the death of Saligram as second guru the movement began to lose its cohesiveness. This had already, in fact, begun in 1884 when Jaimal Singh, a Sikh disciple of Dayal began a parallel organization in the Amritsar district of the Punjab, on the banks of the Beas River. The exact reason for this separation is not clear from the literature, but it has persisted, and another split occurred within the parent group at Agra shortly after 1898. Although there was considerable sharpness between these rival groups as the century ended, each nevertheless was demonstrating a vitality which has proved prophetic for the movement's growth into the twentieth century.[47] Of Dayal, the

[44]Farquhar, op. cit., p. 167.

[45]Frederick Max Mueller, *Ramakrishna: His Life and Sayings* (London: Longmans, 1898), p. 20.

[46]Mathur, op. cit., pp. 38-44.

[47]Mathur, who describes his book as "the first attempt to write a critical history of the Radhasoami Faith from its origin to date," (p. vi) asserts confidently that the faith is stronger than the split. (p. 163) There is some difference as to when the beginning of the

first teacher, Mathur states, "One has to admit that his teachings are confined to spiritualism alone. He has not touched
national problems anywhere in his writings and is indifferent to
other social problems except the caste system and dominance of
priests."[48] Saligram, the second teacher, he identifies as "a
cautious reformer who believes in gradual but steady progressive
change."[49] He opposed caste distinctions in devotional activities, but elsewhere saw both the privileges and responsibilities
which one's caste indentity provided. He spoke for the equality
of women, opposed *purdah*, and worked for women's education.

F. SUMMARY

To conclude this review of movements prior to and contemporary with that begun by Ramakrishna and Vivekanand, we
note a variety of responses to the Western presence which
began to pervade the Indian atmosphere in the nineteenth
century. 1857 was a pivotal year in seeing more Indian initiatives for reform emerge. But, particularly in Bengal, Western
scientific rationalism, social practice and organizational detail
appeared to an elite core to provide the models by which India
might be remade. The early slavish dependence on these models
was receding as the century matured, but the enthusiasm of
some westernizing circles continued to offend the orthodox,
with considerable divisiveness resulting. Others sought to
insure continuity with the past through a respect for tradition,
but by the close of the century their timidity in reform cost
them the allegiance of younger militants. Theosophy's revivalism had what appeared to many Indians to be preposterous
added teachings, and the Arya Samaj seemed overly severe,

---

splits can actually be dated, and some difference of focus as well,
between Mathur, who sees them as occurring later, into the 1900s,
and Philip Ashby, *Modern Trends in Hinduism* (New York: Columbia
University Press, 1974, chapter four, whose briefer treatment focusses
on the Beas group, seems to date that split earlier. Mark Juergen-
smeyer has a draft copy of his article, "Radhasoami and the Revival
of the Sant Tradition," which addresses these issues, also, but from
which I am not free to quote.

[48]Mathur, op. cit., pp. 44, 45.
[49]Ibid., p. 63.

advocating a kind of fictionalized Vedism rather than Hinduism and lacking in religious warmth. No movement appeared to satisfy Justice Ranade's criteria for social, political and religious idealism and to combine them with a mass appeal, unless we identify foretastes in the first glimmerings of a national religious idealism. But into this situation a personality appeared which seemed to incarnate many of the deepest aspirations of the Indian soul, and the subsequent interpretations of this man's genius sought to relate his insight to the particular problems raised by the encounter of India and the West as the twentieth century dawned. This man was Ramakrishna.

CHAPTER
FOUR | The Ramakrishna Movement

A· Ramakrishna: Childhood and Sadhana*

"If one takes into consideration Ramakrishna's life only up to 1875 or so, when he first came into contact with modern educated Bengal, it is difficult to place him in any particular age: he seems so immune from any contemporary influences."[1] At the time, his *sadhana* complete, it seems particularly auspicious that his meeting with Keshab Chandra Sen should have occurred, for by that acquaintance the circle of his influence began to expand. The first public notice of Ramakrishna in a periodical of the time appears to have been in an article by Keshab in the *Indian Mirror* of March 28, 1875, titled, "A Hindu Saint." Describing their first encounter, Keshab reported, "We met a sincere Hindu devotee and were charmed by the depth, penetration and simplicity of this spirit. The never-ceasing metaphors and analogies in which he indulged were as apt as beautiful."[2] It was no momentary fascination, for the relationship between them deepened; each was to have a significant influence upon the other.

While Keshab's circle before this time had become broadly cosmopolitan, Ramakrishna had been immersed in village India, in the vast sea of its saints and sages, its ancient

*Sadhana may be literally translated, 'meditation.' In its conspicuous usage with reference to Ramakrishna, it seems better to describe the different stages of his spiritual path or pilgrimage.

[1]R. R. Diwaker, *Paramahansa Sri Ramakrishna* (Bombay: Bharatiya Vidya Bhavan, 1964) p. 63.
[2]Ibid., p. 252.

myths, legends, and customs. Ramakrishna's pilgrimage had taught him to treasure the wealth of the Hindu tradition by personally striving to realize truth through its varied paths. As we trace the steps of his *sadhana* we are impressed with the tradition's breadth and with the comprehensive character of Ramakrishna's experience of it.

Gadadhar (Ramakrishna) was born late in the marriage of Kshudiram and Chandradevi Chatterjee, a poor, pious farming couple living in the village of Kamarpukur in Bengal. They were worshippers of the boyhood form of Rama, the family deity for many years, made more venerable by the discovery by Kshudiram of a salagrama stone (fossilized shell) associated with Rama. There were auspicious visions and portents before the birth of Gadadhar in 1836, particularly vouchsafed to his mother, who had a warm, generous nature.[3]

The boy early attracted the attention of others by his winning, playful spirit and his gift of mimicry. He was much in demand as a boy for his artistic facility in dramatizing the myths and legends of his people in local festivities. The incorporation of this childish gift into a mature religious vocation is unusual; as we shall see, the extent to which role-playing, specifically, was used in his spiritual quest by Ramakishna would seem unique. Another mature propensity, his easy passage into *samadhi* (a trance state which produces enlightenment) is traceable to his early sensitivity to beauty as well, and his extreme suggestibility to any possible reminder of the divine presence. He went into his first trance at age six or seven on the sight of a flock of snow white swans in the sky. This stimulation to his already strong disposition for worship, enactment of the sacred stories, and meditation made progress in school difficult. His brother Ramkumar, thirty-one years his senior (there were five children; Ramakrishna was the fourth), used his talent for conducting ceremonies and teaching the scriptures to augment the family income for a time, especially after the father's death when Ramakrishna was seven. But Ramkumar's talents were not enough in demand in the village, so he went to Calcutta to start a Sanskrit school. At sixteen Ramakrishna, partly

---

[3]Swami Saradananda, *Sri Ramakrishna the Great Master* (Madras: Sri Ramakrishna Math, 1952), pp. 35-41.

to further his schooling, joined Ramkumar. Ramakrishna, however, was still averse to what he termed "bread-winning education," and much of his time was spent in spiritual pursuits little reached by the more modern aspects of Calcutta culture.

When the new Kali temple at Dakshineswar just north of Calcutta was dedicated in 1855, the donor, a wealthy widow, the Rani Rasmoni, had trouble getting a priest to officiate at the central shrine because of her *shudra* origins. The temple complex, conceived as an ecumenical shrine within Hinduism with separate shrines for Shiva, for Radha-Krishna, and—the largest of all—the goddess Kali an impressive building constructed over an eight year period—no Brahmin would serve as priest. In her search for an officiant, she discovered Ramkumar, a Brahmin, also, but with less of a caste bias, and prevailed on him to take the position. The image of the goddess was duly installed amidst great festivities in 1855, and Ramkumar began his temple service, with Ramakrishna gradually overcoming his own reluctance and joining him there. For a time the youth would eat his food outside the temple precincts, down by the Ganges, with purifying water from the sacred river, or beneath the *panchavati* (five trees sacred to Tantric practice). Later he was to ignore caste restrictions in significant ways and much of his larger spiritual visions was certainly catholic, but the official biographies do not disguise his Brahmin mentality as a youth. Soon he was to become deeply attached to the temple, was asked to attend to the worship in the Radha-Krishna temple, and then, perhaps with the failing health of his older brother, was requested to conduct the worship in the central shrine to the goddess, Kali. With his brother's death a year after he had come to Dakshineswar, this responsibility devolved entirely on this twenty year old youth.

An almost alarming intensity of desire for the saving vision of the goddess began soon to surface. Perhaps his brother's death also triggered his behaviour, but the formal initiation which certified him to conduct the worship was not nearly satisfying enough for him. He was in an agony of longing for the inner presence of the goddess, beyond her image before which he was continually transfixed He became so immersed in his personal services to the image that he was incapacitated for the

conduct of the rituals and complaints were voiced to the Rani
Rasmoni, the temple donor. Upon witnessing his devotional
ardor, however, she felt that the purpose for which the temple
had been built had already been realized. Still, the vision did
not come until, in the darkest of dark nights at its absence,
Ramakrishna was at the point of impaling himself on a ceremo-
nial sword in the temple. This forced the issue, and the transforming vision came. Bliss flooded over him, and from that
point, the emotional tone of his life, where it ranged beyond
that of most men, was one of elation rather than despair.[4]

In the first stages of his *sadhana*, Ramakrishna, with an internalized image of the Mother, was his own spiritual guide. As
his own guru, however, he had such unconcern for his surroun-
dings and mundane matters that those close to him feared
for his psychic health. Although Bengal affords abundant
precedent for devotional ardor approximating madness, his
family was not thereby reassured, and in obedience to his
mother's wishes he went home for over a year, married a young
girl of five and generally became in their eyes more stabilized.
He had directed his family to the home in a neighbouring
village in which his bride would be found, and following the
marriage or betrothal, she remained with her family till the age
of eighteen.

Returning to Dakshineswar, he continued in his devotional
fidelity to Kali until a noted Tantric practitioner, the Bhairavi
Brahmani, appeared on the scene. She led him for three years
through the sixty-four disciplines of the Tantric path (the right
hand Tantric path, significantly, with certain of the more
socially suspect parts undertaken symbolically), regarding him at
an early meeting as a powerful spiritual person, and an incarnation of Chaitanya. He later regarded this as a valid but dangerous path, not advisable for most. He was next led through

---

[4]Ibid., pp. 140-141. Ramakrishna doubtless had this in mind when
he observed later, "One must force one's demands on God. One
should be able to say, 'O God, wilt thou not reveal thyself unto me?
I will cut my throat with a knife.' This is the *tamas* of *bhakti*." While,
then, he could accept this quality in himself and legitimize it for
others, he relegated it to the lowest stage of *bhakti*, the tamasic.
Quotation from M (Mahendranath Gupta), *The Gospel of Sri
Ramakrishna* (Madras: Sri Ramakrishna Math, 1964), p. 119.

Vaishnava paths, first with the child form of Rama, his family deity, by an itinerant teacher, Jatadhari. The childhood penchant for role-playing began again to surface as he continued for some time in adoration of a doll image of the boy Rama, which he carried with him constantly. Another Vaishnavite pattern adopted was the *madhura bhava* or sweet mood, worshipping Krishna as Radha. Once more his genius in merging into the adopted role was intense. He assumed the dress and manner of life of a woman for several months; both to relate to the beloved Krishna, and also, by his own account, to overcome the idea of sexual difference and any trace of lust.

He was next initiated into Advaita, the veneration of the divine beyond name and form. This, apparently, was rather rare in Bengal at the time, and it was difficult for Ramakrishna to purge his mind of the various divine images which had so flooded him. He felt that he needed permission from his still pre-eminent internalized mother, Kali, for this step, however, and this was secured. Tota Puri, a naked ascetic and his guru in the Advaita path, assisted him in gaining the necessary focal point of concentration by literally imbedding a piece of glass in his forehead. He was then astounded when Ramakrishna stayed in the *samadhi* which followed for three days. Ramakrishna became convinced through this experience that all the *sadhanas* took the aspirant toward the non-dual plane, which in turn produced in his mind a still wider catholicity. He soon desired to know something of spirituality beyond his native Hindu tradition, and was initiated into the practice of Islam by Govinda Ray, attaining *samadhi* with Islamic visions after three days of seeking to divest his mind of anything Hindu. Still later, after having a fellow read the Bible to him for a certain period, he also received a vision of Jesus.

His mother was with him in Dakshineswar for the last twelve years of her life, from 1865. And when he returned for a time to his village he again saw his wife, now fourteen, and spent some time in teaching and educating her. She came, then, to Dakshineswar four years later and lived with him for over a year, sharing his vision of what their relationship should be. During this time, neither experienced desire; instead, as the final stage of his *sadhana*, called the *shodasi*, Ramakrishna learned to worship the divine through the body of a woman, whom he continually sought to think of as Mother, natural mother, or sister.

The varied stages of his *sadhana* occupied twelve years; he was now ready for his mature mission.

B. RELATIONSHIPS WITH THE BRAHMOS AND WITH HIS DISCIPLES

Keshub, again, was the primary vehicle of Ramakrishna's coming to the attention of educated Bengal. The richness of the relationship which ensued between Ramakrishna and Keshub is unfortunately marred somewhat by the partisan claims of the followers of each, which have persisted, as to who influenced whom. This tendency was already noted in a Vaishnava journal in 1893, which cites a mutual irradiation.

"Keshub Chandra Sen used to tell his friends that he was gradually making him (Ramakrishna) a convert to Brahmoism; Ramakrishna, on the other hand, told us that he was gradually bringing Keshub Chandra back so Hinduism! And this was the motive which led them to meet so often. As a matter of fact, both were right and they influenced one another. It was Ram krishna, who with his powerful mind, succeeded in convincing Keshub Chandra that there was much in Hinduism that was not to be found in other religions. And it was Keshub Chandra who taught Ramakrishna to take every good thing of every religion. At first, Ramakrishna was a pious Hindu devotee; under Keshub's teaching, he became a cosmopolitan in view."[5]

It may be objected that Ramakrishna's experiments with Islam and Christianity antedate his relationship with Keshub, as they appear to have done. Both men had a disposition to inquire beyond the limits of their own tradition. Their inquiry certainly led them to a different manner of appropriating the truths resident in other faiths, however. Ramakrishna's was almost exclusively mystical, based on his intuition of the nature of Islam and Christianity with very little interaction with their representatives, institutions or literature. This is in no

---

[5]Sankari Prasad Basu and Sumil Bihari Ghosh, eds., *Vivekananda in Indian Newspapers*, 1893-1902 (Calcutta: Dineshchandra Basu Basu Bhattacharya and Co., 1969), p. 298 (quotation from *Amrita Bazar Patrika*).

way to question the depth of the experience, for the observer must have regard for the specific character of his intention, i.e., to experience the truth resident in these faiths. However one may assess the authenticity of his reported experiences, his resolution in pursuing them is clear. But Keshub's travels to the West, his education, use of English, wide relationships with Christian leaders including close working ties with Unitarians, make eminently credible the Vaishnava journal's suggestion that Keshub could have communicated larger measures of ecumenical impression to Ramakrishna. In the same manner, it would seem beyond refutation that Keshub's own devotional nature began to blossom, and with more characteristically Hindu expression, particularly toward the Mother, from his association with Ramakrishna.[6]

An early vehicle by which Keshub shared Ramakrishna with his fellow Bengalis was in publication of a ten page booklet of Ramakrishna's sayings, entitled, in Bengali, *Paramahanser Ukti*. Among numerous references to his friend in the New Dispensation magazine of Keshub's branch of the Brahmo Samaj, one says, "Paramahansa is serving as a marvellous connecting link between the Hindus and the New Dispensation Brahmos. Representatives of both are seen blended together in common meetings."[7] Perhaps both were able to discern in Ramakrishna, in a very deep sense, the Mother lode of Bengali religion.

The official biographies detail many meetings between Ramakrishna and the Brahmos of each group, often in festival occasions. And if the reader imagines that Brahmo gatherings might ordinarily be rather sober and restrained, as might accompany a more philosophical and rational approach to the one God, he would miss the mark. At least in the company of Ramakrishna, these meetings contained many ecstatic aspects, with singing, dancing in free abandon of devotional bliss. But the same official biographies express the feeling that Keshub and the Brahmos generally were too westernized to follow

---

[6]For a thorough exploration, from a Brahmo, perspective of the relationship between the two, see G. C. Banerji, *Keshab Chandra and Ramakrishna* (Allahabad: Indian Press, 1931).

[7]Diwakar, op. cit., p. 255.

Ramakrishna fully. He began to long, instead, for a circle of
his own intimate followers, and these began to appear in about
1879, typically preceded by a vision. This was particularly intense with Naren (later Vivekananda). The two were vastly
different in temperament and background, for, as Nirvedananda
writes, "As opposed to Ramakrishna's delicate physique and
almost feminine grace, Naren, with his strong and athletic
build, was Promethean in vigour and thoroughly masculine in
deportment....a true-born Kshatriya."[8] Later Vivekananda
was also to contrast their prevailing spiritual paths, stating
that externally he was all *jnana*, the intellectual marg or way,
and that Ramakrishna was all *bhakti*. But the relationship
between them, each liberated the strong but latent opposite tendency, bringing wholeness.

Vivekananda was born as Narendranath Dutt on a Hindu
festival day, January 12, 1863, when Ramakrishna was in his
twenty-seventh year. His pious mother, guided by a vision,
dedicated him to Shiva, the god of ascetics, but if that temperament was part of his spiritual make-up, so, also, from his
paternal model, was that of *bhoga*, or enjoyment. Naren's
father was a lawyer, a cultured man of affairs, sophisticated in
his knowledge of the arts, with a particular interest in Islamic
culture. He was generous to a fault, but little interested in
religion. On his death it was discovered that the family had
been living beyond his means and that Naren, the eldest, would
have to leave Presidency College which he had been attending
and seek work.

This precipitated a crisis which had already been building
in him from the time he first met Ramakrishna. Religious inquiry alternated with a stance of philosophical skepticism, imbibed from his deep immersion in his classes. But in one of the
two accounts of his initial meeting with Ramakrishna his ex-

[8]Swami Nirvedananda, "Sri Ramakrishna and Spiritual Renaissance,"
article in *Cultural Heritage of India*, Vol. 4, ed. by Haridas Bhattacharya (Calcutta: The Ramakrishna Mission, 1956), p. 693. In fact
Naren belonged to the Kayastha caste, rather numerous in Bengal,
with the traditional occupation of clerks and letter writers. This gave
them special access to English education and government service, with
many ranked with the Bengal *bhadralok*. Even with this status, however,
they were still ranked as upper-class *shudras* by traditional categories.

plicit spiritual character was evidenced. He states that he addressed to Ramakrishna the question which he had put to many a religious sage, "Sir, have you seen God?" Instead of the usual evasions or qualified responses, Ramakrishna's was amazingly direct: "Yes, my son, I have seen God, just as I see you before me only much more intensely."[9] Stunned by the prompt and unambiguous reply, he was drawn to discover the source of such assurance. In another account, however, their acquaintance came when Ramakrishna asked Naren to come to Dakshineswar after having heard him sing at the home of a friend. Naren, who was eighteen and had just begun his university career, brought some of his fellow students with him. Deeply moved by his singing Ramakrishna passed into ecstasy. Naren continues:

"After I had sung he suddenly got up, and taking me by the hand, led me to the north verandah, and closed the door behind us. We were alone. Nobody could see us. . . .To my great surprise he began to weep for joy. He held me by the hand and addressed me very tenderly, as if I were somebody he had known familiarly for a long time. He said, "Ah! You have come so late. Why have you been so unkind as to make me wait so long? My ears are tired of hearing the futile words of other men. Oh! how I have longed to pour out my spirit into the breast of somebody fitted to receive my inner experiences!" . . . . He continued thus sobbing the while. Then standing before me with hands together he said, "Lord, I know that you are the ancient sage Nara, the incarnation of Narajana, reborn on earth to take away the misery of humanity," I was amazed. "What have I come to see?" I thought. "He ought to be put in a straight-jacket!" . . . But I remained outwardly unmoved and let him talk. He took my hand again and said, "Promise me that you will come to see me again alone, and soon!"

Naren promised in order to free himself from his strange

[9]Romain Rolland, *Prophets of the New India* (London: Cassell and Co., 1930), pp. 177-178.

host, but he vowed within himself never to return."[10]

The rest of the visit was quite normal. Ramakrishna treated his visitor with simple and familiar kindness as if nothing had happened. Ramakrishna discoursed on spiritual matters to the total group, and the wisdom of his words seems to have modified Naren's earlier resolve not to come again to Dakshineswar, for a month later he was back. Despite his defenses, the encounter was still more bizarre, with Ramakrishna causing him to pass into a trance at his touch. On this and similar occasions soon after, Ramakrishna later related that he had probed the depths of Naren's consciousness at the time concerning his spiritul past and the work he had been born to do. He was satisfied with his young friend's potentiality for greatness.

Drawn as he was by Ramakrishna's spiritual magnetism, Vivekananda's intellect rebelled, being repulsed in particular by Ramakrishna's ecstasies in worshipping Kali. He was given freedom to test his doubts, however, and the relationship deepened, to the consternation of some of his associates and teachers in the colleges, such as the rationalist Brojendranath Seal, who later wrote of what he witnessed:

"I watched with intense interest the transformation that went on under my eyes. The attitude of a young rampant Vedantist-cum-Hegelian-cum revolutionary like myself towards the cult of religious ecstacy and Kali-worship may be easily imagined and the spectacle of a born iconoclast and free-thinker like Vivekananda, a creative and dominating intelligence, a tamer of souls, himself caught in the meshes of what appeared to me an uncouth, supernatural mysticism, was a riddle which my philosophy of the pure reason could scarcely read at the time."[11]

The relationship seems to have been sealed in the aftermath of Naren's father's death. Discouraged by employment prospects, concerned for his family's welfare, Naren nevertheless had the strong desire to enter the monastic vocation. Seeking the counsel of Ramakrishna, he was directed to the temple of

[10]Ibid.
[11]Nirvedananda, op. cit., p. 693.

the Goddess, where her spiritual presence became powerfully
real to him. Returning, he had forgotten his own concerns,
and was told to go again. When the same thing occurred, it
seemed to confirm his calling to become a monk, but he needed
reassurance from Ramakrishna that his family would be cared
for. Told that they would not have luxury, but that they would
have enough, he felt free to assume his religious quest. The
order of monks begun shortly before Ramakrishna's death in
1886 saw the leadership pass from Ramakrishna to Vivekananda,
in response to the will of the master. Shortly before his death,
in a vivid scene, Ramakrishna had called Naren to his side.
After being absorbed in ecstacy for a time, Naren heard him
softly say, "Today I have given you my all, and now I am only
a poor fakir possessing nothing. By this power you will do infinite good to the world, and not until it is accomplished will
you return."[12] Still earlier Ramakrishna had indicated to his
favorite disciple that his mission was not to be that of the lonely
isolated *sannyasin*. When Naren implored his *guru* to show
him the way to *nirvekalpa samadhi* or ultimate bliss, he was
given a surprisingly sharp rebuke by his gentle master, "Shame
on you!" Ramakrishna exclaimed. "I never thought you so
mean as to be anxious for your own salvation only whereas you
have powers to do so much good to mankind!"[13] The direction
of the monastic calling had been given, and now the mantle of
leadership had been passed. Naren was not the only disciple;
there were other monastics and householders, but his preemin-
ence was clear, even when he was absent from Bengal for years.

C. VIVEKANANDA'S CONTINUING PREPARATION
AND FIRST WESTERN VISIT

Two years were spent by Vivekananda in consolidating the
newly found monastic order in Baranagore, and in the next
three years most of his time was occupied in visiting the holy
places of India and in treks to the Himalayas, following the
paths "hallowed by the ascetics and seekers of spiritual truth in

---

[12]Ibid., p. 687.
[13]R. C. Majumdar, *Swami Vivekananda: A Historical Review*
(Calcutta: General Printers and Publishers, 1965), 1. 19.

India since time immemorial."[14] But in 1891 he changed his course, traveling through modern India, learning, preaching and teaching. His travels climaxed at the tip of south India, where he swam out to an isolated rock now known as Vivekananda Rock. Here, looking north, he envisioned the whole of India before him in its great agony of suffering. An intensity of compassion welled up in him, and his intuition of his own mission began to flow through him as well. The sleeping leviathan, India, must be aroused. He remembered his master's saying that "religion is not for empty bellies," and vowed to consecrate his life for the liberation of his countrymen.[15]

In a speech in Madras he indicated that his mission must now lead him to the West, where he felt that he could secure material help for his people and preach the truths of his own tradition. That the Parliament of Religions was to be held in Chicago that year, 1893, seemed incidental to him at first. Delegates had been selected over a year previously, so he came without credentials, as the representative of no party or sect within India, but considering himself a spokesman for the whole of his country. He received considerable encouragement and modest financial support for the venture. But he arrived in Chicago in mid-July, discovering that the Parliament was not to begin till September 11. After wandering through the World's Fair for a few days in childish delight, he realized that his funds would be exhausted before that time. Without credentials and a nearly empty purse, he cabled a religious society in Madras for help, but, his independent spirit in coming having given affront, he was told in indirect reply, "Let the devil die of cold!" Even in July this was cold comfort, so Vivekananda, hearing that one might live more cheaply in New England, took a train to Boston to stay till the Parliament would open.

On the train he providentially met a wealthy woman who invited him to stay at her home, where he was soon introduced to the Harvard Sanskrit professor, J. H. Wright. Wright was much impressed with the young swami, arranged lectures for him, and upon learning that he had no credentials to attend the Parliament, was quoted as saying, "To ask for your credentials

[14]Ibid., p. 24.
[15]Ibid., p. 31.

is like asking the Sun to state its right to shine."[16] Wright addressed a letter to the chairman of the committee in charge of delegates, saying again extravagantly, "Here is a man who is more learned than all our learned professors put together."[17] After several weeks in the Boston area, then, armed with this letter of introduction, Vivekananda returned to Chicago and appeared late in the afternoon of the first day's proceedings at the newly opened Art Institute on Michigan Avenue. Records from the press are clear; he was indisputably one of the leading figures of the Parliament.[18] His simple but impassioned initial words of greeting, "Sisters and brothers of America!" caused hundreds to rise from their seats to applaud what seemed the real keynote of the assembly.[19] With his unique gifts and commanding presence, "the cyclonic monk of India" was immediately launched into fame, speaking twelve other times at the Parliament.

Extensive tours followed in the United States, but acclaim alternated with anger, for Vivekananda had become disenchanted with the nation whose circus atmosphere and material achievements had first dazzled him, and his invectives against it were often harsh. Once when he was to lecture on Ramakrishna in Boston, the sight of the crowd, composed of men of affairs, so repelled him that he changed his subject and raged furiously against a civilization represented by such foxes and wolves. Hundreds noisily left the hall and the press was

---

[16]Eastern and Western Disciples, *Life of Swami Vivekananda* (Calcutta: Advaita Ashrama, 1960), p. 297.

[17]Ibid.

[18]*The New York Herald* termed him "undoubtedly the greatest figure in the Parliament of Religions." Majumdar, op. cit , p. 49. There are other superlative tributes to Vivekananda's impact, but it was clearly not a one-man performance. Other favorites also emerged, among them two others from South Asia, Protap Chander Mozoomdar of the Brahmo Samaj and Dharmapala of the Mahabodhi Society.

[19]Rolland, op. cit., p. 37. For other records of the Parliament, with complete texts of all the major speeches, see J. H. Barrows, ed., *The World's Parliament of Religions*, two vols. (Chicago: The Parliament Publishing Co., 1893), and Walter Houghton, ed., *The Parliament of Religions and Religious Congresses at the World's Columbia Exposition* (Chicago: F. T. Neely, 1893).

furious.[20] But his occasional outbursts were tempered by his feeling for what was truly great in America, and its scientific advance, its immense expenditures for public welfare, its industrial and artistic achievements continued to amaze him. His preaching on the larger issues of universal religion attracted many followers, and caused his founding of the first Vedanta Society in the West in New York City in 1895.

Although Rolland comments that his work in America had more lasting effect, Vivekananda felt more at home in Europe, particularly in England, where he visited twice for several months, returning to America in between.[21] Here the knowledge of India was more sophisticated, and he felt less bigotry than in the United States. Moved by the heroism of England, also, the hatred with which he landed on her soil changed to a feeling of love. It was here as well that his most outstanding disciple from the West, Margaret Noble, became his follower, later to be known in India as the beloved Sister Nivedita. That he apparently made no effort to establish permanent societies in Europe is difficult to assess. Perhaps, in meeting such scholars as Max Mueller and others, he felt that knowledge of the East was already more disseminated in Europe than in the United States, but Rolland feels that the terrible fatigue which had begun to weigh upon him is also to be taken into account.[22]

There were further vexing vocational dilemmas. How was he, as a *sannyasin*, to maintain his freedom, retaining some detachment from well-meaning friends who would appreciate him, and also from larger groups, whose demands on a popular hero might not accord with his own assessment of his mission? Another problem presented itself in terms of reconciling his original intention in coming to the West with the posture which was rather forced on him by some of his opponents. He had come expressly for two purposes: to bear the message of India's religious and philosophical wisdom and second, to secure funds to help India meet the grave conditions of poverty and deprivation which confronted her. It may be that his detractors, most

[20]Rolland, op. cit., p. 43. Also Swami Nikhilananda, *Vivekananda: a Biography* (New York: Ramakrishna-Vivekananda Center, 1953), p. 66.

[21]Rolland, op. cit., p, 69.

[22]Ibid., pp. 95, 96.

of them Christian missionaries and converts from Hinduism such as Pandita Ramabai, with their followings, forced him largely to abandon the second objective. They attacked Hindu society as being so debased and vile that he was driven to defend it to the point of idealizing its achievements. This posture obviously qualified any appeal which he could make for monetary gifts to alleviate needs in India. To make such an appeal would be to acknowledge a measure of substance to criticisms leveled by the missionaries.

For his Western mission, the Swami turned increasingly from the lecture platform to the establishing of smaller, more intimate groups of disciples. After the New York center was begun, a number of persons joined him at Thousand Islands State Park for a time of close, personal instruction. Two persons, Madame Marie Louise and Leon Landsberg, received their full monastic vows from Vivekananda on this occasion, but their subsequent careers make the wisdom of that step controversial. His words during these days, however, were preserved and published under the titles, *Inspired Talks*, by Miss Ellen Waldo, and these contain excellent vignettes of the manner in which he related to his disciples. Another woman who was present from Detroit later came to India as Sister Christine and served devotedly with the Ramakrishna Movement in its activities in Calcutta. She also relates how he would refrain from offering counsel unless a person were to accept him as a guru. In that event, however, he would assume a very direct approach in guiding the aspirant's spiritual progress. "Friends might have a narrow outlook," she notes, "might be quite conventional, but it was not for him to interfere. It seemed that even an opinion where it touched the lives of others, was an unpardonable intrusion into their privacy. But once having accepted him as their guru, all that was changed. He felt responsible. He deliberately attacked foibles, prejudices, valuations."[23] Mrs. Dutcher, his hostess, a small woman of Methodist background, rather quailed under his frontal assaults. Yet he cultivated no slavish dependence. In harmony with his high assessment of human nature, he thundered, "Stand upon

[23]Sister Christine, in Eastern and Western Admirers, *Reminiscenses of Swami Vivekananda* (Calcutta: Advaita Ashrama, 1961), p. 210.

your own feet. You have power within you." Christine comments, "His whole purpose was not to make things easy for us, but to teach us how to develop our innate strength."[24] When he left the West, he was confident that he was leaving a small core of strong, self-reliant disciples.

D. VIVEKANANDA'S MISSION IN INDIA AND CONCLUDING ACTIVITIES

Returning to India on January 15, 1897, the victor's laurels were showered upon him, particularly at Madras, where his first lecture, "My Plan of Campaign," was directed to the whole of India. He was acclaimed, in borrowed imperial language, as one who had vanquished the West. The Rajah of Ramnad, who had first suggested the idea of the Parliament to the Swami, was quoted in his tribute as saying, "Your Holiness has crossed boundless seas and oceans to convey the message of truth and peace, and to plant the flag of India's spiritual triumph and glory in the rich soil of Europe and America."[25] The hero's welcomes staged at Colombo, Madras and Calcutta were of tremendous magnitude. India's collective national ego obviously received a heady infusion to counter the oppressive weight of negative assessment growing out of her subject status and comparative material backwardness. Now she had something to communicate, a cultural product which Western nations were eager to receive.

For the populace, then, India was a viable entry into the market place of nations only by the assertion of her spiritual supremacy. Vivekananda's early dual strategy, then, in going to the West was now given operational consolidation. India could learn from the West's material achievements, and his letters from America to his brother monks were clearly in the direction of a revised idea of the monastic vocation. His initial letter had criticized the role of the holy men of India: "A million or so of Brahmins suck the blood out of these poor people, without even the least effort for their amelioration—is that a country or a hell?" The Swami went on to speak of his earlier

24Ibid., p. 212.
25Basu and Ghosh, op. cit., p. 134.

vision at Cape Comorin where, "I hit upon a plan: we are so many *Sannyasins*, wandering about, and teaching our people metaphysics—it is all madness...Suppose some disinterested *sannyasins*, bent on doing good to others, go from village to village, disseminating education and seeking in various ways to better the condition of all down to the Chandala, through oral teaching, and by means of maps, cameras, globes. . . ."[26] He held no illusions that his new program would win easy acceptance. Captivated by the energy and vigour of America, however, he was eager to transmit this spirit to his religious associates in India. After extolling America, he would confess, "I have become horribly radical. I am just going to India to see what I can do in that awful mess of conservative jellyfish."[27] Other satirical comments make clear his impatience with time-wasting ceremonials, diverting attention from needed social service and demanding intellectual pursuits. Henceforth, his powers of persuasion having been dominantly asserted, his brother disciples would devote themselves, if not to social reform, certainly to social service of wide ranging character. This ideal was given institutional expression in the beginning of the Ramakrishna Mission in Calcutta on May 1, 1897. Although illness soon set in, he made use of the least respite to increase his work tenfold, preaching throughout northern India, teaching his disciples from the West, consolidating the work of the monastic order, immersing himself in meditation and study.

Another year and a half was spent in the West in 1899 and 1900, strengthening his disciples and beginning new missions, particularly in California, where he stationed Swami Turiyananda who, with Sister Nivedita, had accompanied him on this visit. In California, also, he regained a measure of health. But, although his fire against it now burned low, Vivekananda was still distressed by much of the superficiality which he saw in Western life, as he had on his earlier visit. He said to Nivedita, "Social life in the West is like a peal of laughter; but underneath it is a wail. It ends in a sob. The fun and frivolity are all on the surface; really it is full of tragic intensity. . .Here (in India)

---

[26]Vivekananda, *Letters of Swami Vivekananda* (Calcutta: Advaita Ashrama, 1960) pp. 96, 97.
    [27]Ibid., p. 351.

it is sad and gloomy on the surface, but underneath are care-lessness and merriment."[28]

Thus, after a few months in Europe, he returned once more to his homeland, weary and belonging more to the next world than to this. Yet he remained active until the end, which came almost, so it seemed to his disciples, as an act of volition, at the close of one of his more vigorous and joyous days, which had included three hours of teaching Sanskrit to the novices. In a last affectionate interview with his fellow monks, he spoke of the rise and fall of nations, and said, "India is immortal if she persists in her search for God. But if she goes in for politics and social conflict, she will die."[29] Later in the evening, after a period of meditation in his room, eternal silence fell. He was thirty nine years of age, and his death came on July 4, 1902.

In the person of Vivekananda the waters of witness of his master, Ramakrishna, the village Bengali saint, had impressively washed on other shores. As the first of the Eastern movements to find institutional expression in the West in modern times, it had started with promise by the century's end. Even more, for India, it had ignited a spirit of religious nationalism which was to influence many other persons and movements.

28Sister Nivedita, *The Master as I Saw Him* (Calcutta: Advaita Ashrama, 1923), p. 145.

29Rolland, op. cit., p. 169.

| The Islamic Response

A. MUSLIM DISADVANTAGE UNDER BRITISH RULE

Up until 1857 "Muslim feeling was quite straightforward. It
regarded the British as usurpers of Muslim power; and it aimed
to break that power and restore Muslim ascendancy."[1] The
interpreter, Ralph Russell, goes further to explain this strategy
as reflective of a widespread feeling that for centuries, "We
Muslims ruled the whole country; bearers of the true faith
prevailing by sheer superior dynamism."[2] For the Hindu
population, the British presence meant simply the replacement
of one alien rule by another, with perhaps the possibility of
more stability. For Muslims, issues of faith were involved.
Opposition was dictated on grounds of Islamic law, not simply
to British rule, but to all things British, their culture, their language, their dress, their education, etc. Naravane's useful book,
Modern Indian Thought, rhapsodizes on the harmonies which he
sees to have existed between, first, Islamic and Hindu cultures,
stating, "Each tradition had within itself the latent seeds of the
other. The result was a wonderful synthesis of culture and
thought—a synthesis that is unparalleled for its richness and
appeal."[3] The disparate reactions by the Hindu and Muslim

---

[1]Ralph Russell, "Strands of Muslim Identity in South Asia, "*South
Asian Review* October, 1972, p. 22.
[2]Ibid.
[3]V.S. Naravane, *Modern Indian Thought* (Bombay: Asia Publishing
House, 1964), p. 11

communities to the British presence, however, betray that whatever synthesis had resulted was superficial. If such a synthesis of culture and thought had indeed been effected in the minds of the people, they would not have responded to the new, third factor, in so opposite a fashion. The thesis here advanced is that Hindus had no roadblocks comparable to those of Muslims against trafficking on the highway to modernity that the British offered. Thus, until some of their strategies began to be modified late in the nineteenth century, the Muslim community's fortunes were to languish at many levels under British rule.

Communalist tensions between Hindus and Muslims, latent, comparatively, under Mughal rule, now began to be accentuated with possibility of better redress for the Hindus. These included issues such as cow slaughter, the playing of processional Hindu music before mosques, coincidence of Muslim and Hindu festivals, obstruction and desecration of each others places of worship and festivals, struggle for government posts, and extraterritorial sympathies of Muslims. Muslims were alerted to the dangers for their status as early as the Permanent Settlement under Cornwallis, when the setting up of Hindu *zamindars* began to modify Islamic law. The injection of secular law, in small doses, followed until the province of the old Muslim legal structure was reduced to personal and civil law. Earlier, for example, Muslim law had made apostasy from the Islamic faith punishable by death, and where that penalty was not invoked, disinheritance was. Hindu law had similarly provided for disinheritance for apostasy. In 1832, however, this disability was removed in Bengal and in 1850 for the country at large. In that climate, Christian schools and government schools alike began to thrive. And, although the latter had to maintain an exclusively secular approach, traditional Muslim schools felt a threat from each.[4]

Extra-territorial aspects of Muslim identity, mentioned above, were also easier to maintain under Mughal rule. Urdu, which Percival Spear calls "the graceful daughter of Persian and Hindi,"[5] may be interpreted as a cultural bridge in some

[4]Maheswar Karandikar, *Islam in India's Transition to Modernity* (Westport, Conn.: Greenwood Publishing Corp., 1969) pp. 137—139.

[5]Spear, op. cit., p. 120

ways, but it allowed Muslims to preserve Persian motifs exces-
sively, inhibiting true Indianization. Imagery in Urdu literature
was drawn exclusively from Persian precedents in what may be
seen as "an instinctive effort to preserve in a culturally alien
and hostile milieu its own cultural roots, signs, symbols and
insular patterns of expression. . .It was a desperate unconscious
clinging to the origins of the symbols of Muslim India's cultural
experience which had begun abroad, and an instinctive escape
from the fear of submergence into the Hindu cultural milieu,
with its strange gods, its almost pagan love of the actual Indian
nature, its startling realism, and its tempting fragrance and
rhythm."[6] As late as 1896 Yaquinuddin Ahmad wrote, "In
Calcutta Hindus are called Bengalees by every Muhammedan,
who has never traveled beyond the Maratha Ditch (built to
protect the city against Maratha incursions in the eighteenth
century), as if such Muhammedans by the fact of their professing
the faith of the great Arabian prophet have a right to be non-
Bengalees."[7] *Shariff* (noble) identity for Muslims, particularly
in Bengal, lay in the crucial factor of having ancestry traceable
to Persia, its near-Eastern Neighbors, or at least to the immediate northwest of India. Many thus claimed fictitious foreign
lineage.

Indigenization was not crucial, then, so long as political
realities were congenial to the Muslim cause. But when the
ruling power as well as the culture was alien, the Islamic population was severely disabled. It is estimated that at the time of
Cornwallis Muslims held 75% of government jobs, but this
began swiftly to erode. By the middle of the 19th century the
British, witnessing this, the theologically dictated illiteracy for
Muslims, etc., sought to initiate compensatory measures, but by
the century's end, only 6% of the Muslim male population was
literate as against 10% of the general population.[8]

[6]Aziz Ahmad, *Studies in Islamic Culture in the Indian Environment*
(Oxford: Clarendon Press, 1964), p. 253.
    [7]Asim Roy, "The Social Factors in the Making of Bengali Islam,"
South Asia: Journal of South Asian Studies, August, 1973, p. 27.
    [8]Y.B. Mathur, *Muslims and Changing India* (New Delhi: Trimurti
Publ., 1972), p. 65.

B. Sir Sayyid Ahmad Khan

Sir Sayyid (1817-1898) was to the Muslims as Rammohun
Roy had been to the Hindus. Born into a family of Mughal
officials, he entered the British judicial service. His activities
for reform among the Muslim population centered around
Delhi, as those of Rammohun Roy did around Calcutta.
Although there is no evidence of direct dependence by Sir
Sayyid on Rammohun Roy and the Brahmo Samaj, he relates
how, as a boy, he saw Roy in Delhi just before the latter left
for England. The event was perhaps prophetic, for Sayyid was
not intimidated as were most of his kinsmen from working with
the British. From the time of his brief employment with the
East India Company till his own visit to England in 1869,
almost forty years after Roy, he seems to have been moving
personally to that conclusion, and the conviction that for other
Indian Muslims the only road to modernity lay in cooperation
with the British.

To make his case, Sir Sayyid had to employ a strategy
similar to that of Rammohun Roy, also; to demonstrate convin-
cingly that Islam was not inherently antagonistic to reform in
consonance with the modern scientific spirit. His opponents,
again similarly, in the *ulema* (official interpreters of Islamic
law), were no less formidable than those Roy faced, also, among
the leaders of Hindu orthodoxy. He approached his task philosophically, mustering evidence that Islam, like Christianity,
coming from a Jewish heritage with exposure to Greek intellectual currents, was dependent on reason as well as revelation.
Reason was the vehicle whereby its insights could be applied
practically to the discoveries of modern science.[9] Just as it could
incorporate, discriminately, these new developments, so it must
do its theological homework, identifying itself as distinct from
Hinduism. Only through these twin strategies could the Islamic
community in India move out of the lethargic swamps in which
it had become mired. C.F. Andrews, analyzing the movement
which emerged from Sir Sayyid's initiatives, coined the phrase,.
"The Delhi Renaissance," which, in response to English education, was largely scientific, whereas that in Bengal had been.

[9]Spear, op. cit., p. 225.

more literary.[10] Sir Sayyid's philosophical base for such a
renaissance was his ranking of nature alongside of, or even
above, the Quran itself as a source of authority.[11] But he was
concerned to relate the two and again, reason provided the
linkage. Earlier sayings and traditions based on the Quran were
no longer binding; in his new interpretation of it, modern
thought could serve to contemporize the ancient wisdom.

Mathur states: "According to Muslim law, as espoused by
the Sunnis of the Old School, it was not lawful to learn English
or the language of any other non-Muslim people except for the
purpose of answering letters, or of combating the religious
sentiments of those people."[12] For Sir Sayyid, the only way that
Muslims could resume their rightful place and advance culturally
and economically was through English education, and this was
a pivotal platform in his reform movement. Aligarh College,
which he founded in 1875, became a primary expression of this
interest, and was the acknowledged center, subsequently, of
Muslim modernism. Many young Muslims entered government
service from its ranks, and competent, sophisticated defenses of
Islam emerged also. As with the Bengali reformers, women's
rights also occupied a major portion of his concern. His energies
were primarily channeled into providing for women's education
and with the giving up of *purdah*, or the veiling and relative
isolation of women.

Surendranath Banerjee met Sir Sayyid in 1877, and subsequently paid tribute to Aligarh University as "the center of
that culture and enlightenment which has made Islam in India
instinct with the modern spirit, and aglow with that patriotic
enthusiasm which augurs well for the future solidarity of Hindus
and Mohmmedans."[13] His point concerning the University is
surely valid, but other efforts of Sir Sayyid cannot with san-
guinity be judged to have contributed to Hindu-Muslim
solidarity. These efforts crystallized around his opposition to
the Indian National Congress. This movement, he felt, would

---

[10]Christian W. Troll, *Sayyid Ahmad Khan: A Reinterpretation of
Muslim Theology* (New Delhi: Vikas Publishing House, 1978), p. 150.
   [11]Ibid., pp. 218-222.
   [12]Y.B. Mathur, op. cit., p. 54.
   [13]Banerjee, op. cit., p. 46.

ultimately result in the departure of the British; majority rule which would follow would be Hindu rule, and this would be much more destructive than the British *raj* for Muslims. Thus Sir Sayyid, "the tallest among the Muslims," maintained a studied silence on the Congress when it was founded in 1885, but this changed to militant opposition. Earlier he had "stood and moved like a colossus on the Indian political scene as the champion of modernity, reform and Hindu-Muslim coopera-tion."[14] This negative assessment of his stance observes that Muslim participation in Congress had grown during his silence, but that with his opposition, first voiced in a speech in Meerut early in 1888, this began to decline. "Now suppose," he declared, "that all of the English and the whole English army were to leave India. . .then who would be the rulers of India? Is it possible that under these circumstances two nations—the Mohammedans and the Hindus—could sit on the same throne and remain equal in power? Most certainly not. It is necessary that one of them should conquer the other and thrust it down."[15] Thus, although he did not give credence to the possibility of the separate nations, his policies were to contribute to their greater separation. He counseled Muslims, then, to keep themselves aloof from "the political uproar of the Congress," desiring the continuance of English rule "forever."[16] While Muslims had, in the immediate aftermath of the Mutiny, an unfavorable image in British eyes, with Sir Sayyid's leadership there began to be fostered before the century's end what has been termed the powerful "myth of the loyal Muslim."

C. THE WAHABI AND KHILAFAT MOVEMENTS

India under British rule presented the first large scale challenge to the question, "Can Islam be practiced under non-Islamic rule, and can Muslims pledge their loyalty to such a rule?" Obviously, for Sir Sayyid, the answer was affirmative, and many others followed in this interpretation. British rule, if it did not fully

---

[14]S.K. Mittal, "Muslim Attitude Towards Indian National Congress (1885—1900)," *Journal of Indian History*, April, 1976, pp. 143—144.
[15]Ibid., p. 147.
[16]Ibid.

provide for conditions of *Dar-ul-Islam* (House of Islam, literally) was at least neutral toward the practice of religious Islam. The mosques were open, Ramadan and pilgrimage were possible, prayer could be freely practiced, and Muslim personal law was enforced. The government could not be assailed as corrupt and degenerate; human rights, by most standards, were being pursued. In addition, scientific education could advance the lot of man at a new and rapid pace.

But again the question, "Could Islam really be apoliticized?" Kenneth Cragg is doubtless correct that "Islam never abandoned the axiom that it was made to rule.[17] Accordingly, a truer reading than that of Sir Sayyid for the Indian situation was that it fulfilled the conditions of *Dar al-Harb*, the antonym of *Dar al-Islam*, a country that needed to be liberated, "the unpeaced abode." It was yet to be brought into conformity and concord with Islam. Wahabi and Khilafat movements rose out of this conviction.

The Wahabi movement originated in the eighteenth century, being named for its founder in central Arabia,' Abd al-Wahhab. He belonged to the Hanbali school, strictest of the four canonical schools of law, and he began a movement to purify Islam, to return it to the unadulterated Islam of the Prophet and the Quran. This meant cutting through and abolishing accretions such as pilgrimage to shrines, veneration of saints, the cult of intercession, etc. It was clearly iconoclastic, and was to form, for much of the Islamic world, a zealot temper and tone which was to continue into the twentieth century. In India the concerns of the Wahabis, sects from that source such as the Faraizis in Bengal, and related movements such as that of Titu Mian, also in Bengal, and of Sayyid Ahmad Barelvi, all assumed a militant stance. Followers of these groups were *Mujahidins*, "those who engage in *jihad*," or the holy war, and it included those who were preparing for such war and those who were in some way supporting persons active in such war. But in India it soon had practical expression; it did not remain theoretical. Its particular expression in Bengal was to mobilize the political consciousness of the Muslim peasantry, ruthlessly exploited

[17]Kenneth Cragg, *The House of Islam* (Belmont, Calif.: Dickenson Publishing Co., 1969), p. 82

under the Permanent Settlement, in addition to the specific concerns to purify Islam and oppose British rule.

Sayyid Ahmad Barelvi, perhaps the most prominent among the leaders of this cluster of movements, drew his primary inspiration from the thought of Shah Wali-Ullah rather than the Wahabis. Wali-Ullah, of Delhi, had sought to channel the streams of Sufi heritage into traditional Islam, and generally to check the spiritual decadence which he observed in Islam in eighteenth century India. This movement, like that of Sayyid Ahmad Khan, was based on the necessity of *ijtihad*, or speculative reconstruction of Islamic law, but along more fundamentalist lines than those of the great nineteenth century reformer. This was a more lean and Spartan movement, rejecting the peripheral, the eclectic, the syncretic and the heterodox. It meant also the repudiation of Indian, Persian and Christian customs which were contrary to the teachings of the Prophet.

Both Sayyid Ahmad and Titu Mian, his Bengali disciple, were slain in abortive attempts at *jihad* in 1831, but the former had chosen Sikh territory on the northwest frontier as his target, where the rule unlike that of the British, was brutally anti-Muslim, denying them freedom of worship, honor and security.[18] It has been suggested that the British may have actually connived in the diversion of this popular militant movement to its Sikh neighbors. Sayyid Ahmad had set up a small theocracy in the frontier hills and had occupied Peshawar before his defeat. Similarly, Titu Mian controlled three districts of Bengal and defeated several small British detachments before he was defeated and slain by a major British expedition. "It is a curiosity of history," writes a 1964 interpreter, "that over a century before the creation of Pakistan, two miniature Muslim states struggled to emerge vaguely on the horizon of realization, if only for a very short while and against overwhelming odds, but ideologically linked together, and situated in the same Muslim majority areas which today constitute Pakistan."[19]

The British were to see some of these movements surface again throughout the century. When they succeeded the Sikhs in the Punjab, for instance, sixteen years after the death of

---

[18]Aziz Ahmad, op. cit., pp, 214 — 217.
[19]Ibid., p. 217.

Sayyid Ahmad, they were opposed by a small and ineffective band of his followers, armed with little else than the belief that their leader had not really died, but would return to guide them if they took up the battle once more. More significant than these outcroppings were the persistent rumors late in the nineteenth century of pan-Islamic, or Khilafat movements, subversive to the British raj in India. In 1895 these rumors took shape in the activities of Maulvi Hidayal Rasul, who stated that the 22 crore of Muslims in the world were the army of the Sultan and that their spiritual allegiance to him in any conflict must take precedence over temporal loyalty to the British or any other national rule. This seemed to generate little response, but sufficient for the British to imprison him for a time. Another movement with clear pan-Islamic overtones, the Nadwal-ul-Ulema, similarly had little success with its political goals, but was able to cultivate certain educational objectives. The most successful effort of right-wing Islam in the nineteenth century, however, came in the founding of the rival university to the one founded by Sir Sayyid at Aligarh. The Deoband school became the center for Muslim puritanism and political freedom in the latter part of the century. Persons from this persuasion could countenance cooperation with Hindus in Congress activities, for instance, feeling that with India declared *Dar al-Harb*, the primary theocratic end should be to drive the British from the country. Opposition by the orthodox crystallized against Sir Sayyid when he supported the British in action against Arab interests in Egypt and, accordingly, against pan-Islamic interests. The Turkish caliphate for him was a dead cause, and cooperation with British imperial power had more to offer to Indian Muslims.[20]

D. THE AHMADIYAH MOVEMENT

The extravagant claims of Hazrat Mirza Ghulum Ahmad, founder of this movement, from the time of his mission's beginning at the age of 54 in 1889, mark this as a distinctly different phenomenon. The claims are messianic, and they purport to find in him the fulfillment of the longings of the peoples of four

[20]Karandikar, op. cit., pp. 146—149.

major faiths. His second successor, Hazrat Mirza Bashiruddin
Mahmud Ahmad, details them in vivid manner.

Our belief is that all these things (messianic hopes) are to be
found in the Holy founder of the Ahmadiya Movement,
Hazrat Mirza Ghulam Ahmad (on whom be peace and the
blessings of God) whom God raised for the reformation of
the present age. He claimed to be the Messiah for the Christians, the Mahdi for the Muslims, Krishna or the Neha
Kalank Avatar for the Hindus, and Mesio Darbahmi for the
Zoroastrian. In short, he was the Promised Prophet of every
nation and was appointed to collect all mankind under the
banner of one faith. In him were centered the hopes and
expectations of all nations: he is the Dome of Peace under
which every nation may worship its Maker; he is the opening
through which all nations may obtain a vision of their Lord;
and he is the centre at which meet all the radii of the circle.
It is ordained, therefore, that the world shall find peace and
rest only through him. Being a Persian by race he was then
the Promised One of the Zoroastrians; being an Indian by
birth he was the Promised one of the Hindus; being a Muslim
by faith he was the Promised One of the Muslims; and having
come in the spirit and power of Jesus, bringing remedies for
the reformation of the social evils prevailing in Christian
countries—evils, which have laid an intolerable burden on
the backs of the Christian nations—having been born under
a Christian Government, and also having defended the
honour of Jesus against the attacks which have been levelled
at it for hundreds of years, he was entitled to be recognized
as the Promised One of the Christians.[21]

These beliefs are not simply those which the followers developed, reflecting on who their master had been. Mirza, in
making such assertions himself, said, "I would be guilty of an
injustice were I to conceal the fact that I have been raised to

[21]Hazrat Mirza Bashiruddin Mahmud Ahmad, *Ahmadiyyat, or the
True Islam*, (Rabwah, Pakistan: Ahmadiyya Muslim Foreign Missions
Office, 1959), pp. 10-11.

this spiritual eminence."[22] As might be expected, however, the movement encountered considerable opposition to what were regarded as its fantastic pretensions. Some followers clustered, chiefly in the Punjab, the place of origins, and the movement appeared by the century's end to have expansionist, missionary possibilities. While it insisted that it was thoroughly a Muslim movement, it did not accept the status of simply another Muslim sect, however, but claimed that it was the true Islam.[23] The primary basis for this conviction is that, although it regards the Quran as a complete book, it also insists on new and continuing revelation. In this way, it regards itself as open to receive truth from many sources, including other faiths, science, and, of course, through the Promised One himself, the founder of the movement.

Much of the movement's dogma centers around its revelatory claims. Here Mirza, the founder, felt that many persons, mostly Muslims, had prophetic insights in differing degree. His were, of course, perfected, and he exercised these in what proved at times distressing ways, interpreting the prophetic role as giving concrete predictive powers. Farquhar relates how his common practice of publicly predicting the death of certain individuals caused such an uproar that the British in 1899 ordered him to cease and desist, to which, under extreme pressure, he agreed.[24] By and large, however, the movement's relations with the British were extremely cordial. As much as Muslims could be, perhaps, the Ahmadiyahs sought to be apolitical. Loyalty was due the ruler if he did not expressly violate his subjects. *Jihad* could only be countenanced as defensive strategy. In the midst of such communal discord, the pacific record of the Ahmadiyahs is rather striking.[25]

Another facet of Ahmadiyah teaching which distinguishes it

---

[22]Mirza Ghulam Ahmad, *The Philosophy of the Teachings of Islam* (Washington: 1953), quoted in Aziz Ahmad and G.E. Von Grunebaum, *Muslim Self-Statements in India and Pakistan, 1857-1968* (Wiesbaden: Otto Harrassowitz, 1970), p. 80.

[23]Hazrat Mirza Bashiruddin Mahmud Ahmad, op. cit., p. 21.

[24]Farquhar, op. cit,, p. 143.

[25]Humphrey J. Fisher, *Ahmadiyyah, A Study in Contemporary Islam on the West African Coast* (London: Oxford University Press, 1963), pp. 79-82.

from orthodox Islam has to do with its interpretations of Jesus. Jesus, for Mirza and his followers, did not die on the cross, with subsequent resurrection and ascension, but lived on to teach further in the East, finally dying a natural death and being buried in Srinagar, Kashmir. He had actually been crucified, taken down from the cross supposedly dead, but was revived. This, for the Ahmadiyahs, was to honor him as a prophet, but to disallow the claim that Jesus was God or that he continues to live with God.[26] Orthodox Muslim belief held to the ascension, but for Mirza and his disciples, Jesus renounced such claims to divinity in fully identifying with the human condition. The Second Coming, then, is not the bringing back to life of Jesus, but God raising up the Messiah from among the followers of Muhammed, which has occurred in the person of Mirza.[27]

In summary, British rule posed critical problems for the Islamic community in India which it met in a variety of ways. Clearly it felt itself initially under the threat of how to continue faithful adherance to Islamic practice while politically subservient to an alien power. Cooperation was inhibited on theological grounds, and Muslims began to lose ground in public service, education, etc. Men such as Sir Sayyid began to reverse this tide, however, in providing schools and a philosophical basis for them. Culturally, an Islamic renaissance was initiated, and Muslims began to feel that they could thrive, not merely survive, under the British. The greater threat, as Hindu nationalism began to surface, appeared to be from the prospect of living under the majority religion with the British deplaced. Seeds of Islamic communalism had begun to flourish by the end

[26]Farquhar, op. cit., pp, 138—142. See also statements by Hazrat Mirza Bashiruddin Mahmud Ahmad and Mirza Ghulam Ahmad, the founder, in Ahmad and von Grunebaum, op. cit., pp. 77-84.

[27]Ibid., H.A.R. Gibb, *Modern Trends in Islam* (Chicago: University of Chicago Press 1947), reviews the Ahmadiya Movement very briefly and then judges, "On the whole, the Ahmadiya are an unimportant element in Indian Islam." (p. 62) Their record of peaceful behavior, their messianic claims and missionary practices, may, however, mark them as a significant enough departure to merit further academic inquiry. One such recent work is Spencer Lavan's *The Ahmadiyah Movement: a History and Perspective* (Delhi: Manohar Book Service, 1974). This was originally presented as Lavan's thesis at McGill University.

of the century. While sectarian movements within Islam sought, on occasion, to live the implications of the faith without regard to the political scene, mainstream Islam in India, as elsewhere, defined its existence in significant measure with reference to the ruling powers.

CHAPTER SIX

Beginnings of a Buddhist
Renaissance

A. A Continuing Buddhist Presence
in the Northeast Frontier

A variety of factors culminating in the Moslem invasions
around A.D. 1000 caused the virtual eclipse of Buddhism in
India, the land of its birth. A handful of Buddhists, however,
persisted in their religious identity in Bengal, confined to the
northern districts of Darjeeling and the southeastern districts of
Chittagong. "Bengal became a laboratory, so to say, where
Buddhism mixed with esoteric beliefs and practices."[1] Tantric
rites and rituals in these hill regions modified the abstract
character of some Buddhist philosophy, and its monastic aspects
largely vanished. But with these alterations and the addition
of Hindu deities and customs, at least a barely recognizable
form of Buddhism persisted, taking some hold on the life of the
people. In the 1860s a Buddhist priest from Arakan landed in
Chittagong with the express purpose of awakening these followers to a purer form of Buddhism. Some success was visible,
at least among the more educated, many adopting the surname
Barua and claiming descent from kings of Arakan. Monasti-
cism was reinstituted, and every Barua had to be initiated to the
life of the *sramana* (monk) for at least seven days. Of those
remaining in the order for a longer period, a lifetime vow of

[1]Benoy Gopal Roy, *Religious Movements in Modern Bengal* (Santine-
ketan: Visva-Bharati, 1964), p. 171.

celibacy was required only in the highest of four orders, the
Mahathera. Others could receive permission to leave the
order and marry.[2] While the movement did not penetrate the
interior, it did provide a vehicle whereby certain intellectuals
could expand their awareness of the historic teachings of
Buddhism.

B. THE BENGAL BUDDHIST ASSOCIATION

Kripasaran Mahathera, born into the Chittagong Buddhist
community in 1866, was dedicated by his mother to the Buddhist
order after his father's early death, and at age sixteen was initiated into the monastic life. As his formal teaching neared
completion, he toured the Buddhist holy places of India with
his teacher. "As he saw the holy spots, he painfully realized
the decadent state of Buddhism in India. He took a vow to
resuscitate Buddhism once more on Indian soil."[3] Coming to
Calcutta with money and against strong opposition, he began
to preach his faith. Ekeing out an existence in the traditional
Buddhist fashion of begging, door to door, he was often discouraged, but in 1892 he founded the Bengal Buddhist Association,
having received backing from a few Calcutta intellectuals such
as Sir Ashutosh Mukherjee. In the same year a modest library
and *vihara* were also built in Calcutta. Stated objects of the
Association were 1) "To maintain and improve the social, religious, educational, civic and economic status of the Buddhists
of Bengal and of the rest of India in general; and 2) to resuscitate Buddhist culture and to propagate the tenets of the
Buddha and principles of Buddhism."[4] By the century's end,
attempts had begun to start branches in other Indian cities
such as Darjeeling, Shillong and Lucknow, and attention was
being given to the consecration of a shrine at Kushnagar in the
district of Gorakhpur, where archeologists had determined
that the Buddha had died.

[2]Ibid., p. 170.
[3]Ibid., p. 165.
[4]Ibid., p. 167, 168.

C. Buddhist Themes in Literature

The modest Buddhist revival began to stimulate interest in details concerning the life and teachings of the Buddha. This was advanced by a number of writers, as in Girish Chandra Ghose's *Buddhadev Charita*, Nabinchandra Sen's *Amitava Kabya* and Satyendranath Datta's *Buddha Purnima* and *Buddha Baram*. But as in so many other literary areas the Tagore family were leaders here, also. Rabindranath's older brother, Satyendranath, explored such themes in his *Buddha Dharm*. And Rabindranath himself, commenting on the Dhammapada, noted the need for further such study. "Materials of different shades of Indian thought and culture are confined in Buddhist literature, and due to the lack of intimacy with them the entire history of India remains unfulfilled. Being convinced of it, cannot a few youths of our country dedicate themselves for the restoration of the Buddhist heritage and make it a mission in life?"[5] In part, Tagore did this himself, stating, upon visiting some of the Buddhist holy shrines, "I am a disciple of the Buddha. But when I present myself before these holy places where the relics and footprints of the Buddha are found, I come in touch with him to a great extent."[6]

Three of Tagore's dramas, *Malini*, *Chandalika* and *Natir Puja*, are based on Buddhist stories, and in the latter there is a particularly captivating incident which conveys a Buddhist insight. When Princess Ratnavali in this play ironically expresses her disregard for Bhikku Upali, born a barber, Sunanda, the son of a milk man and Sumita an untouchable, the nun Utpalavarna replies, "Oh, Princess! They are all equal in caste; you have no knowledge of the yardstick of their aristocracy."[7] Themes such as these were also given currency by men such as Vivekananda, who related that as a child he had had a vision of a serene, shaven-headed figure, with staff and begging bowl. The image so frightened the astounded Naren that he rushed from the room. Yet he reported to a fellow disciple years later that he almost instantaneously regretted having done so, for the

---

[5]Sudhamsu Bimal Barua, "Rabindranath Tagore and Buddhist Culture," *Bodhi Leaves* pamphlet, 1961, p. 4.

[6]Ibid., p. 7.

[7]Ibid., p. 18.

figure never appeared again, and Naren felt that it might have communicated something to him verbally. Reflecting, he seemed to make an identification. "I now think that it was the Lord Buddha that I saw."[8] In any case, Vivekananda drew considerably on the Buddha's example for his own understanding of the role of the monk in the Ramakrishna order, particularly for its model of social service.

D. Boyhood and Youth of Dharmapala

The most significant movement of Buddhist revival in the nineteenth century, the Mahabodhi Society, is almost the single-handed story of one man, Dharmapala, born David Dewavitarne, son of a wealthy furniture manufacturer in Ceylon. His background in that Buddhist country was to give him confidence to address Buddhist nationals of differing persuasions concerning what he regarded as the heart of the Buddhist message. It also enabled him to confront the Western presence, with the threat that it posed to religious loyalties and feelings of national and personal worth. In Ceylon, the challenge was frontal, and inevitably experienced in his time at an early age. Buddhist schools, in Dharmapala's childhood, had been closed by the government, and since few government schools had been started in their place, missionaries of Christianity had stepped in to fill the void. Dharmapala was sent to a Roman Catholic school nearby, but careful attention was given at home to his Buddhist education, also. While he admired his teachers at school, he was revolted by their meat-eating, and reports a particularly traumatic experience in seeing one shoot down a bird. In contrast to the "wine-drinking, meat-eating, and pleasure-loving faculty members at school, the *bhikkhus* who habitually graced his home were characterized as "meek and abstemious."[9] Two famous Buddhist leaders whom he knew intimately from childhood were the Venerables Sumangala and Gunananda. Sumangala was noted as high priest of the Temple

[8]Swami Pavitrananda, *Talks with Swami Vivekananda* (Mayavati, Almora: Advaita Ashram 1946), p. 122-123.

[9]Anagarika Dharmapala, *Return to Righteousness*, ed. by Ananda Guruga (Ceylon: Government Press, 1963), p. 685.

of the Sacred Footprint of the Buddha on Adam's Peak, founder and head of the Buddhist College in Colombo. Gunananda was a golden-tongued orator who responded to Christianity's attacks on Buddhism and developed aggressive counter-measures in return. Given this strong reinforcement of his ancestral faith, he strongly resented a favorite teacher who honestly confessed, "We came not to teach you English but Christianity."[10] The same teacher had beaten him when he absented himself for Wesak observances, but when Wesak came each of the next two years, he was absent again, with the same punishment being administered.[11]

His resistance to the above approach was strengthened in 1880, with the arrival of Theosophist leaders Madame Blavatsky and Colonel Olcott, who volunteered to assist in responding to the Christian gauntlet. Dharmapala's own education had been interrupted because of this controversy, initiated when a group of Christians had attacked a Buddhist procession going by their school. Almost on the eve of his completion of a secondary program, his father withdrew him from the school. Given his appetite for learning, Dharmapala began to explore a wide range of interests on his own, also accepting employment as a government clerk. By this time, when he was 18, Blavatsky and Olcott revisited Colombo. At the time of their first visit four years earlier, he had been fascinated with them; now he was in a position to relate to their message vocationally. His father gave permission for him to go with the group to Adyar in India, but the night before departure, the father had a dream which caused him to withdraw his approval. Olcott concurred with the father and the Venerable Sumangala, being called in, did also, but Madame Blavatsky said, resolutely, "That boy will die if you do not let him go. I will take him with me anyway."[12] In the face of this formidable assertion, the opposition withered.

In Adyar, however, Blavatsky did not press the advantage by yielding to Dharmapala's expressed desire to study the more

[10]Ibid., p. 684.
[11]Bhikshu Sangharakshita, *Anagarika Dharmapala: A Biological Sketch* (Kandy, Ceylon: Buddhist Publication Society, 1964), p. 14, 15.
[12]Dharmapala, op. cit., p. 687.

occult aspects of Theosophy. Rather he was told, "It will be much wiser for you to dedicate your life to the service of humanity. And, first of all, learn Pali, the sacred language of the Buddha."[13] He soon returned to his government post for two years and then changed his volunteer activity in the evenings to full-time, vocational work for the Theosophists in Ceylon. This continued for some five years, until 1891, when he returned from a lecture tour with Olcott to Japan. At this time he wanted to return more specifically to the concerns of his ancestral faith, and he began publishing the *Buddhist* from Ceylon early that year.

Almost immediately, however, he felt something missing in his own experience of Buddhism, and he began a pilgrimage to the historic shrines in India, with the most hallowed destination being Buddh Gaya, where the Buddha, almost two and a half millenia earlier, had won enlightenment. But that which he had anticipated as a high spiritual moment provoked another sort of trauma. The shrine was in poor state of repair, grown up in weeds, with stones fallen. What maintenance was provided came from an owner who seemed to him not respectful of the shrine's historic import. That a Shaivite, with the rites and rituals which he sponsored, the symbols which he had allowed to have recently engraved, should have custody over this sacred domain, seemed to Dharmapala clearly out of accord with its Buddhist origins.

This moment became pivotal for the young man, who was given his rallying call for what might be termed the first modern Buddhist ecumenical movement, soon to be institutionalized in the Mahabodhi Society. He began the Society almost immediately, in May, 1891, with the following stated objectives:

The consolidation of the different Buddhist nations, the restoration of the sacred Buddhist sites in India, the rehabilitation of the Law in the land where it originated, the founding of an international missionary training college for young men in Benares or Buddh Gaya . . .[14]

[13]Ibid.
[14]Ibid., p. 708.

E. The Shrine at Buddh Gaya

The Society's headquarters were located, as they have remained, in Calcutta, and Dharmapala began publishing the *Mahabodhi* (great enlightenment)*Journal* the following year. He was not dependent so much as the Bengal Buddhist Association had been on public support, since the family fortune was available to undergird his new ventures. As the Society's name, and that of the *Journal* implies, the location at Buddh Gaya was always pre-eminent as the center of the Buddhist world, and its acquisition and restoration, at least in the early years, the central objective. It appeared that this would not be difficult of attainment, for support was not wanting from influential quarters. One of these, Sir Edwin Arnold, author of *The Light of Asia*, wrote in the following terms to Arthur Gordon, then administering the government of Ceylon:

> Buddhagaya is occupied by a College of Sivite priests who worship Mahadeva there and deface the shrine with countless emblems and rituals foreign to its nature. That shrine and the ground surrounding it remain, however, government property, and there would be little difficulty after proper and friendly negotiations in procuring the departure of the Mahant and his priest, and the transfer of the temple and its grounds to the guardianship of Buddhist monks from Ceylon.[15]

The *Behar Times* agreed, stating, "So far as the general body of Hindus are concerned, we believe there is no serious objection to the temple being restored to the Buddhists; indeed, such a course would be most natural and proper."[16] *The Hindu*, described as "the leading organ of the native community of South India," said

> We quite agree with our contemporary of the *Indian Mirror* (whose editor, Narendra Nath Sen, remained an eloquent advocate of Buddhist revival in India) in thinking that the clear duty of the Hindus is to repudiate both the Mahant and his utterly unjustifiable attitude toward the Buddhists of

[15]Ibid., p. 610.
[16]Quoted in the *Mahabodhi Journal*, June, 1894, p. 17.

late. Buddhism is a religion of which the people of India
have good reason to be proud . . . When Buddhism spread
to other countries, it carried with it a reverence for India,
its place of origin. When it comes back now to us after its
conquests of millions of human beings, it is not proper that
we should give it a slap on the cheek. We ought to welcome
it back and accord to its votaries our sympathy and help.[17]

The same journal, repeating this counsel, said, "Educated
Hindus need not hesitate in helping Buddhism to find a commanding and permanent footing once more in their midst and
to live in invigorating and mutually purifying amity with Hinduism itself."[18] But the Mahant had his supporters also. The
editor of *Light of the East*, another Hindu journal, observed
that, "The orthodox position of the Hindu community view
with much alarm the increasing influence of Buddhism in
India."[19] As this alarm was sounded, it made a much difficult
task to secure the Mahabodhi Temple from the Mahant than
Dharmapala and Arnold had first suspected. Considerable
bitterness and rancor surrounded the rivalry for the shrine in
the early year, whose Buddhist character the British had recognized in a marble slab erected at the time of some efforts in
restoration in the 1880s, noting it as "the holy spot where
Prince Sakhya Sinha became a Buddha."[20]
This hostility became particularly intense on February 25,
1895, when Dharmapala sought to install an image of the
Buddha given him in Japan for that purpose. The Mahant had
first agreed to its installation, but then only if it were first installed in a "life-giving ceremony" constituting it as a Hindu deity.
On the fateful morning, however, Dharmapala felt inspired to
proceed with the installation without the Hindu ceremony.
Just after this was done, so a lengthy article in the *London Times*
reported, a mob of 500 Hindus gathered and ordered its removal. The Buddhists refused, and governmental officials inter-

---

[17]Ibid., p. 22.
[18]Anagarika Dharmapala, *History of the Mahabodhi Temple* (Calcutta: Mahabodhi Society, 1900), p. 11.
[19]*Mahabodhi Journal*, November-December, 1895, p. 53.
[20]Dharmapala, *Return to Righteousness*, p. 588.

ceded, trying to restore calm. But then the Hindus regrouped and removed the statue, throwing it outside on the ground, while the Buddhists remained seated in contemplation.[21] The statue was subsequently removed to a Burmese rest house nearby when the government supported the Mahant's position, whereupon, for some years, he sought its removal from there as well. This was not achieved, but despite widespread support from influential quarters for the Buddhist character of the site, Dharmapala and his friends experienced repeated frustration in their efforts at Buddh Gaya.

Even in its frustration, however, the efforts at Buddh Gaya provided a continuing impetus for a "return to the roots" motif which guided the movement's ecumenical endeavors. Dharmapala sought to challenge the various national Buddhist *sanghas* (monastic communities) to share in the promotion of shrine rebuilding, fund raising, etc., to encourage pilgrimages to the historic locations in India, and to stimulate missionary activities directed back toward the Buddhist homeland, aiming at its eventual conversion. These larger goals were advocated by some whom Dharmapala sought to enlist in the Buddh Gaya restoration, but who would admit of no small concerns. He was impatient with the leadership in Thailand for their timid support for the Buddh Gaya project, since their identity as a Buddhist nation placed them in such a crucial position. But they, in turn, tutored Dharmapala into a greater breadth for his mission. Prince Rajanubhav, in a Calcutta interview with Dharmapala, said:

Mr. Dharmapala, Buddhism is not brick and mortar; you may spend a *lakh* of rupees in buying up the sacred temple, but before you do that, you ought to prepare the way for the dissemination of the moral truths of Buddhism. You should establish a headquarter in Calcutta immediately and set to work . . . . Concentrate your efforts on the diffusion of knowledge, for that constitutes Buddhism.[22]

[21]*Mahabodhi Journal*, November-December, 1895, p. 54—57.
[22]Dharmapala, *Return to Righteousness*, p. 847.

F. THE MISSION BEYOND INDIA

Dharmapala seems to have followed the above counsel in founding his Society and in publishing the *Mahabodhi Journal* so
soon. He was soon thrust into the limelight of leadership in
the Buddhist community of Ceylon, also. Events were underway in America for the gathering of the World's Parliament
of Religion in Chicago in 1893. In Ceylon, the correspondence
from Chicago had been addressed to the young editor of the
Mahabodhi Journal, who forwarded the invitation to attend to
the Venerables. When these declined, Barrows, the Chairman
of the Parliament, asked Dharmapala himself to attend. Although the suggestion did not come from them, it does not
appear that the elders in Ceylon objected and when an American
friend and a Ceylonese now living in America volunteered to
pay his passage, Dharmapala consented to go as a spokesman
for Southern or Theravada Buddhism.

As mentioned in Chapter four, Dharmapala, with Vivekananda, Mozoomdar, etc., became a favorite at the Parliament.
In his initial address, Dharmapala indicated that Dr. J.H.
Barrows, the convenor, might prove to be an American
Ashoka, calling a conference whose representatives might go
out in the spirit of the Buddhist monks whom Ashoka commissioned two millenia earlier, combining their gentleness with
the meekness of Jesus.[23] But after missionary addresses by
Christian leaders did not seem to him to reflect that same
meekness, Dharmapala asserted himself, also, in a more
forceful manner. He criticized certain missionaries for their
arrogance in Asian countries, going with a Bible in one hand
and a rum bottle in another. It was offensive to his Buddhist
sensitivities, also, that despite the youthful energy of the city
of Chicago, the Parliament had to be held in a city of great
slaughterhouses, and he did not wish this quality of civilization
to be exported to the Orient.[24] Still, he was appreciative of
the possibilities which the Parliament had offered, and was
hopeful that these might be realized.

He had traveled west to the Parliament, being greeted by

[23]Houghton, op. cit., p. 60, 61.
[24]Ibid., p. 608.

Sir Edwin Arnold in Britain, who went with him to visit Lord Kimberley, Secretary of State for India, on behalf of their interest in Buddh Gaya. After the Parliament he returned by the Pacific, stopping in various Buddhist countries to enlist support for his ecumenical objectives. Holmes Welch gives a fascinating account of difficulties which he encountered in Shanghai, which are indicative of the dimensions of the road-blocks in the path of his grand idea. An appeal for support had apparently been agreed to by Buddhist leaders there shortly after Dharmapala's arrival in late December, 1893. But the following morning these same leaders asked to be released from their promise. Welch follows Franke and De Groot in believing that this was because Dharmapala had approached them on behalf of a society.

A dread of everything in any way resembling association weighs most heavily on the State and its whole officialdom . . . . All societies, therefore, except those of fellow clans-people, have to be exterminated, like the sects, with strangul-ation, flogging, and banishment. If involvement in an indig-enous Chinese society was dangerous, it was much more so to get involved with a foreign society, especially one in India, a country that had been conquered by the same red-faced foreigners who were now threatening to conquer China—and whose representatives had accompanied Dha-rmapala to help him make his first contact.[25]

Timothy Richard, one of these representatives, however, knew of more liberal spirit among the Buddhist leaders, and he invited this man, Yang Wen-hui, to come from Nanking to meet with Dharmapala. At the time Yang also rejected the idea of Chinese pilgrims visiting Buddhist locations in India, but in subsequent correspondence over some years, came to change his mind. Thus Yang, often spoken of as the father of the Buddhist revival in China, may have received a vision of Bud-dhism's still wider mission through this early contact with Dharmapala. Another important relationship for Dharmapala

[25]Holmes Welch, *The Buddhist Revival in China* (Cambridge: Harvard Univ. Press, 1968), p. 7.

was begun on this return voyage in 1893, with Mrs. Mary Elizabeth Foster in Hawaii, who subsequently became an important benefactor for the Mahabodhi Society.

G. RELATIONSHIPS WITH THE RAMAKRISHNA MOVEMENT AND THEOSOPHY

Two of the significant contacts which Dharmapala made at the Parliament were with Annie Besant, soon to come to India as a leader of the Theosophical Society, and with Swami Vivekananda. Indeed, returning to Calcutta, he gathered the brother monks of Vivekananda in a setting with fascinating dynamics. Vivekananda had been somewhat estranged from these men before his departure, and he had remained in the West after the Parliament for more than three years, as it transpired. Dharmapala brought the Bengali monastics together with the first word that they had received directly from the Parliament, preceding by a few weeks their first letter from Vivekananda, who was to become again their leader. After meeting with them, in a Calcutta address on May 14, 1894, Dharmapala's words leave little doubt as to what his message to them must have been.

> There is not only Swami Vivekananda. I have seen his colleagues in the Dackinesore Math, and I say if five or six men go abroad with the liberal ideas of the great master Ram Krishna, I am sure, you will soon bring about a great revival of Hinduism among the millions of human beings in this country. If you organize a missionary propaganda, millions will join you in your great work. Send them to all parts of the world. You have got the key, and the success is in your hands. The best men of England and Germany are now learning the Indian philosophy. Let the great men of Bengal, Rajahs and Maharajahs, help them to form a missionary propaganda. Thus, you will have done your duty to Bengal and your duty to India.[26]

Vivekananda, on his return to Bengal in 1897, was to have

---

[26]Basu and Ghosh, eds., op. cit., p. 389.

no small opposition to his missionary and service oriented version of Hinduism, or Vedanta, Hinduism universalized, as he termed it, but he had a precedent for such activity in Buddhism, and in the recent interpretations of it by Dharmapala. Dharmapala's own missional strategy moved more toward institutional promotion than did Vivekananda's, at least in the early years. The Ramakrishna Mission operated on a "no conversion" policy, speaking, at least in philosophical ideal, of the broad substratum of truth underlying all religions. It sought to promote this truth, and attempted to awaken in persons of all faiths an awareness of this. It was, to be sure, the identification of a mystical core as basic to religion, and that having a Hindu coloration. To see this core as primal in all traditions involves the observer in certain distortions, but at least a wider toleration was promoted by this stance than has generally been evident in promotional strategies of world faiths.

Dharmapala's model looks more familiar to students of Western religions. From an early desire to restore Buddhist historic sites in India, to a vision of ecumenical concern in enlisting the national Buddhist *sanghas* together for this purpose, he moved to a policy of active promotion of Buddhist evangelism, aspiring to the making of converts to Buddhism in India and elsewhere. This, coupled with some apparently unappreciative remarks about Buddhism by Vivekananda, served to widen the space between the two movements. Dharmapala, traveling in America again in 1897, learned of Vivekananda's remarks in a press release from Calcutta. From his diary, we learn of his response:

I find Swami Vivekananda in his lecture had denounced Buddhism in unmeasured terms. For five years I had a great respect for him and loved him for his excellent qualities and I defended him at the risk of my own popularity wherever I went. When the Brahmo Samaj People were against him I defended him in a public lecture at Madras. I spoke about him in the National Congress to over 5000 people, and in the Victoria Hall, and I gave my full sympathy for his work. But when his turn comes to help me he shows his nature. I feel sorry for him He has lost a splendid opportunity. He had friends now, and he has alienated the sympathy of

hundreds from me. Peace to you, Swami, and may you get
a true conception of Buddhism.[27]

Subsequently, in contacts in Boston and New York, Dharmapala had cordial relationships with several Vedantists, including Swami Saradananda from India, and at least one of them,
Mrs. Ole Bull, wrote to Vivekananda objecting to his strong
utterances against Buddhism.[28] Dharmapala also learned of
Vivekananda's ill health, which caused him to excuse him
somewhat. Still, relationships between the two movements
and their leaders never regained the promise of closeness with
which they began.

Similarly, by the century's end, strains were developing with
Theosophy. As important as that connection had been in
Dharmapala's formative years, Theosophy's move to Adyar
involved it in what he regarded as a defense of Brahminism,
caste structures, etc., as well as the incorporation of claimed
Tibetan elements which were offensive to his Theravada stance.
Perhaps as each of these three movements developed institutional
identities, promotional strategies inhibited their cooperative
efforts. Dharmapala was also developing an anti-British feeling
which was not present in the other movements.

The Mahabodhi Society's beginnings, however, were significant in their own right. Efforts were begun to restore historic
Buddhist sites in India, the homeland of the Buddhist tradition.
With that restoration came a new pride in the foundations of
the faith. It was to take time before something of Dharmapala's
vision could be transmitted to other Buddhist countries,
however, each of whom had existed so long without ties to the
Mother Country, having established their own pilgrimage
centers, etc. But the building of bridges back to India was a
way of relating various national Buddhist communities more
closely, also. Dharmapala had shared a vision, and the Buddhist
presence in India, languishing for centuries, was once more
visible.

[27]Dharmapala, *Mahabodhi Journal*, June, 1956, p. 294, 195.
[28]Ibid., p. 296.

| Religion and Nationalism

A. NATIONALISM IN THE TRADITION

Bharat Mata—Mother India: You may go to the holy city,
Varanasi, and see in the temple by this name not the anticipated
altar, shrines and images, but instead, within the spacious sanc-
tuary, surrounded by a brass rail, a huge relief map of the
nation—*Bharat Mata*. How shall we interpret this phenomenon?
Radhakrishnan gives large credence to the criticism which says
"that India did not till recently take to the cult of the nation.
We did not make our country a national goddess, with a historic
destiny, a sacred mission, and a right of expansion. We did not
worship Mother India. . .proclaiming to the people that we are
the finest people on earth, the chosen race of the universe."[1]
Radhakrishnan may be correct in the sense of India as a political entity with a historic mission to expand beyond its borders.
But 'Mother India' is an organic, not a political image, originally,
and in this sense the idea lies deeply rooted in the ancient,
sacred soil of the subcontinent. Natural patterns of ebb and
flow rather than historic, pivotal moments describe the course
which the nation has followed. "The subcontinent is seen as a
product of natural evolution, not a stretch of territory gained
within the struggles of history."[2] As such, the sacred soil motif

---

[1]S. Radhakrishnan, *Eastern Religions and Western Thought* (New
York: Galaxy, 1939), p. 54.
[2]Paul Younger, *Introduction to Indian Religious Thought* (Philadelphia:
The Westminister Press, 1972), p. 28.

fed a stream of insularity rather than expansion; the mission was to nurture, to cultivate, and to guard against contamination. Late in the nineteenth century the idea was still pervasive that to leave the sacred soil was to break with the womb (*garbha*); forfeiture of status within society was often imposed on those who transgressed even briefly in this manner. Vivekananda, returning from the West in 1897 found not only his Western followers barred from the Dakshineswar temple complex, but himself as well.

B. MISSIONAL COMPONENTS

The missional component, however, began to change toward the end of the nineteenth century. Clear religious overtones accompanied the rise of nationalism, as in the following quotation from Vivekananda:

> If there is any land on this earth that can claim to be called blessed *Punya-Bhumi* (sacred soil), to be the land to which souls on this earth must come to account for *karma*, the land to which every soul that is wending its way Godward must come to attain its last home, the land where humanity has attained its highest towards gentleness, towards calmness, above all, the land of introspection and of spirituality—it is India.[3]

Vivekananda's voice did a great deal to swell feelings of national pride, but more overtly political movements sounding a nascent nationalism began a generation earlier. Raj Narain Bose, grandfather of Aurobindo, was affectionately termed, also, "The Grandfather of Indian Nationalism," for his founding of a society for the Promotion of National Feeling in 1866. He also started a national paper and a national school, and his Hindu Mela, first instituted in 1867, was held fourteen times between then and 1889. The society may be considered a forerunner of the Congress[4] in creating an All India outlook and fostering a

[3]Quoted in V. S. Naipaul, *India: A Wounded Civilization* (New York: Vintage Books, 1976), p. 162.

[4]J. N. Vajpeyi, *The Extremist Movement in India* (Allahabad: Chugh Publications, 1974), pp. 34, 35.

spirit of national pride and progress. Similarly the Indian Association previously mentioned, as founded by Surendranath Banerjee in 1876, aimed to foster Hindu-Muslim unity for the masses of India. Banerjee's level of commitment to this movement is indicated by his having attended the inauguration of the Association, although his only son had died that morning.[5] Some of the impetus for this organization derived from *The Hindu Patriot*, founded two years previously by Banerjee's friend, Kristo Das Pal, who began its publication with the statement that attention should be directed to Home Rule for India.[6] This marked a clear change of direction, and coming from what Banerjee called the most influential newspaper in Bengal of that day, the idea seed began slowly to germinate.

Banerjee also observed, "You cannot think of a social question affecting the Hindu community that is not bound up with religious considerations."[7] For a man who worked for Hindu-Muslim unity, such considerations were not always positive, but they did provide much of the content and motivation to achieve the vision of autonomous rule. Initial efforts were timid, simply in the direction of petitioning the benign British despot for a larger share in governance, but the last quarter of the century saw this escalate. Dadabhai Naoroji, long an advocate of co-operation with the European rulers, now began to question the quality of the relationship, suggesting that it could no longer be defended as of mutual benefit, but approximated that of master-slave.[8] Such feelings were gaining currency. The *Amrita Bazar Patrika* of August, 1857, said:

> The people of India have all along consoled themselves with the belief that though they sometimes suffer wrongs at the hands of their Anglo-Indian masters, it is done without the knowledge and sanction of the people in England. The universal belief is that the English in England, unlike a

[5]Ibid., p. 41.

[6]U. S. Srivastava, "The Evolution of the Concept of Swaraj (1885—1906)," in Bisheshwar Prasad, ed., *Ideas in History* (London: Asia Publishing House, 1968), p. 298.

[7]K. P. Karunakaran, *Religion and Political Awakening* (Meerut: Meenakashi Prakashan, 1965), p. 17.

[8]Srivastava, op. cit., p. 299.

portion of their brethren in India, are strictly just, and would
never knowingly allow an injustice to be done. This belief is
on its trial.[9]

The article goes on to anticipate that the forthcoming visit
of the Prince of Wales would enhance, not heal, the mistrust,
that he would come to smooth over differences with gracious
assurances which would have little result.[10]

Surendranath Banerjee, again, expressed his feeling of similar
suspicion that the benign despotism of the British was changing
to benign neglect.

Both Liberals and Conservatives have, from the front benches, uttered the shibboleth that India lies outside party
considerations. Sir Henry Fowler, when Secretary of State
for India, declared from his place in Parliament that every
member of Parliament was a member for India. The sentiment was greeted with cheers, it was palpably so noble and
so instinct with the consciousness of duty to an unrepresent-
ed dependancy. In India, however, it evoked a smile of
incredulity. For we all know that what is everybody's business is nobody's business, and each year the truth is painfully
impressed upon our minds when we read the accounts of the
debates on the Indian budget in the House of Commons and
the empty benches to which the oratory of the speakers is
addressed.[11]

Banerjee however, recognized that a great deal did depend
on the personality of the Secretary of State for India and on
other officials, and he was very enthusiastic, as were Indians
generally, about Lord Ripon as Viceroy of India under Glad-
stone. Both of these identified with popular causes such as the
repeal of the Vernacular Press Act and for the establishing of
the 1882 act on Local Self Government.[12]

[9]Quoted in "Rousselet's Travels in India," *The Westminster Review
and Foreign Quarterly*, April 1, 1876, pp. 416, 417.
    [10]Ibid.
    [11]Surendranath Banerjee, *A Nation in Making* (Bombay: Oxford
University Press, 1963) p. 52.
    [12]Ibid., pp. 58—61.

C. BIRTH OF THE CONGRESS

The pivotal event leading to the birth of the Congress in 1885, even so, was a reform measure, the Ilbert Bill, from which Ripon had to retreat. The Bill provided that Europeans resident in India could be tried for criminal offenses in courts presided over by either English or Indian Judges, and it created a racial turmoil among the colonials. Under the threat of this "White Mutiny" Ripon compromised, and the educated Indians then become incensed, still more following the brief imprisonment of Surendranath Banerjee.[13] The new viceroy, Lord Dufferin, initially gave a guarded approval to the Congress, telling A. O. Hume, one of its active sponsors, that, "as head of the government, he had found the greatest difficulty in ascertaining the real wishes of the people; and that for purposes of administration through which the Government might be kept informed regarding the best Indian public opinion.[14] In effect, then, for Dufferin, the Congress had potential utility both as sounding board and as safety valve. Hume, doubtless, a lover of liberty, wanted more for India than that, and this was credited in that he was President of Congress three times between 1885 and 1900.

D. THE MODERATES

Some of the initial claims made for what the Congress might achieve were asserted on the basis of broad philosophical and religious assumptions, not those peculiar to India. Dadabhai Naoroji, a Parsee, and later the first Indian to be elected to the British Parliament, could transcend Hindu-Muslim communalism in stating that Indians had as their human right the privilege "to inherit the great blessings of freedom and representation."[15] Banerjee, in the year following Congress' birth, stated it more explicitly: "Self-government is the ordering of nature and the will of Divine Providence. Every nation

[13]Vajpeyi, op. cit., p. 41.
[14]Lala Lajpat Rai, *Young India* (Delhi: Ministry of Information and Broadcasting, 1965), pp. 113, 114.
[15]Srivastava, op. cit., p. 298.

must be the arbiter of its own destinies."[16] Even though Congress had begun in 1885 with a mere seventy delegates, messages such as these struck responsive chords. The cry for *Swaraj*, self-rule, had found a natural mouthpiece in the Congress, which swiftly moved beyond Dufferin's hoped for safety valve status.

Moderates, however, prevailed in the early years of Congress. Chief among these, as mentioned, were Justice Ranade and his loyal disciple, Gopal Krishna Gokhale, who continued to stress social reform along with political freedom. Ranade was "a constant figure on the Congress platform as a visitor, and he was the power behind the throne, guiding, advising, and encouraging the Congress leaders in their work."[17] His successor, Gokhale, "with his polished speeches, his parliamentary manner, his facts, and his formidable logic, was the westward-looking Indian's pride."[18] So long as men of this temper dominated, the British presence was not essentially under fire. In the 1890s, however, as Tilak's extremist persuasion moved more into the ascendancy, the Government's position toward Congress began to harden. With Muslim representation dwindling to insignificance, Congress also assumed a more specifically Hindu religious base. Tilak astutely popularized politics in Maharasthra in 1893 and 1895 with the institution of Ganesh and Shivaji festivals. Immune to interference as religious festival, they did in fact, through discourses, awaken a revived interest in the Hindu cultural heritage, but in making a folk hero of Shivaji, fostered a rallying point to mobilize the masses in the cause of political freedom.[19] Valentine Chirol, writing early in the twentieth century in profound disaffection with directions taken by the Congress, called Tilak "The father of Indian unrest," and saw in his apotheosis of Shivaji the creation of a model of murderous treachery.[20] For Tilak the precedent was action not motivated by selfish desire,

[16]Ibid.

[17]Banerjea, op. cit., p. 46.

[18]Spear, op. cit., p. 171.

[19]M. P. Sreekumaran Nair, "B. G. Tilak: The Moderate as Extremist," *Journal of History*, December, 1976, pp. 572, 573.

[20]Valentine Chirol, *Indian Unrest* (London: Macmillan and Co., 1910), p. 41.

as taught in the Bhagavad Gita. Shivaji exemplified this for him and the people of India, similarly, were called on now to exercise the British as the only fitting act of free men.

E. THE MILITANTS

Tilak was charged with sedition in 1897 in the aftermath of the killing of a strong-handed British official who had come to Poona to combat a plague. The assassins of the official, Walter Charles Rand, and an associate, were brothers who seemed clearly to have been influenced by Tilak's inflammatory editorials in his journal, *Kesari*, immediately before the event. While no direct complicity on Tilak's part was ever demonstrated, he was convicted and sentenced to eighteen months of rigorous imprisonment. Almost immediately this exalted him to martyr status, and earned him the universally employed title, *Lokamanya*, "revered by the people," as Gandhi was to be called *Mahatma*, "great soul," in the twentieth century. His conviction inspired nationalist poets like Ram Das to sing:

> Lion-hearted Tilak, let not thy heart sink,
> A nation's heart beats within thine own,
> A nation its tearful eyes uplifts to God—
> For justice for thee and an ancient land.[21]

Tilak had already won the respect of the intellectuals by his Sanskrit scholarship and of the orthodox by his championing of venerable texts. Now he became a popularizer of his country's cause with the young and the uneducated, who could identify with his suffering and sacrifice as his badges of belonging. "Gokhale inspired no such general adulation. India's problems, as he viewed them, would not be solved by rallying numbers around his platform. . .His concern for the plight of the meanest of India's masses was no less intense than Tilak's but the solutions he suggested were never as dramatic, and he lacked Tilak's flair in speech or writing. He could coin no slogans. He saw less hope

[21]Stanley A. Wolpert, *Tilak and Gokhale: Revolution and Reform in the Making of Modern India* (Berkeley: University of California Press, 1962), pp. 102, 103.

for peasant amelioration in religious revival than in economic progress of a steady kind, and by 1897 he had emerged as British India's leading unofficial spokesman for economic reform."[22]

This strategy, obviously, was also of lasting value, but the triumvirate of Bal-Lal-Pal (Bal Gangadhar Tilak, Lala Lajpat Rai and Bipin Chandra Pal) were taking the public by storm at the century's conclusion. The three also symbolized the all-India character of religious nationalism, with Tilak from the west, Lajpat Rai from the northwest and Pal from the Northeast. Lajpat Rai's Hindu origins in the Punjab were diluted by his grandfather's having been a Jain shopkeeper and his father a Muslim "by conviction" as a young man, and under the influence of Sayyid Ahmad Khan. The son as well was a great admirer of Sir Sayyid, but his entry into political life at age 24 was occasioned in 1888 with his "Open Letters to Sir Syed Ahmed Khan," challenging the anti-Congress statements of the Muslim leader.[23] He moved from an early identification with the Brahmo Samaj to the more militant Hindu revivalism of the Arya Samaj. In his mind, the primary task of nation-building was to overcome the deep divisions in Hindu society. If this meant the postponement of efforts at Hindu-Muslim unity and social reform, he was willing to let them be deferred.[24]

Bengal, obviously, had the legacy, earlier mentioned, of Bankim Chandra's militant *Bande Mataram*, and of his novel *Ananda Math*, the first edition of which described a *sanyasi* rebellion against the British. Subsequent editions substituted Muslim rulers for the British as objects of the revolt to avoid charges of sedition, but the appeal of devotion to the Mother Goddess in overcoming fear and attachment to worldly possessions became a primary theme in Bengal political activism. Bankim Chandra died in 1894, but the culture of national courage remained more vigorous in Bengal than anywhere in India. Aurobindo Ghose in 1893 published an extremist attack on Congress for its timidity, stating that the "actual enemy is

[22]Ibid., p. 103.
[23]John R. McLane, *Indian Nationalism and the Early Congress* (Princeton: Princeton University Press, 1977), pp. 336, 337.
[24]Ibid., p. 336.

not any force exterior to ourselves, but our own crying weaknesses, our cowardice, our selfishness, our hypocrisy, our purblind sentimentalism."[25] Vivekananda, also outside of Congress, indeed removed from direct political involvement itself, nevertheless inspired ideals of physical strength and courage with statements counseling the young men of Bengal that, "You will be nearer to Heaven through football than through the study of the Gita."[26]

Bipin Chandra Pal's militancy was slow to evolve, although he had been under the tutelage of Surendranath Banerjee since the early 1880s. His chief preoccupation till his return from the west in 1900 had been his missionary activity for the Brahmo Samaj, but his politically moderate stance was soon to change. He was now on the threshold of reviving the spirit of Young Bengal's radicalism.[27] Again, the religious dimension of political activism in Bengal under his leadership, that of Aurobindo and others, was to take shape around Shaktism, the veneration of the mother goddess in her forms as Kali and Durga. At the century's end, as Donald Smith notes, the country "was the Mother, but not a defenseless female: "Thou art Durga, Lady and Queen, with her hands that strike and her swords of sheen."[28] The judicial restraints of Ranade and Gokhale were no longer captivating and Gandhian ideals of non-violence would be embryonic for another twenty years. The century closed with the prospect that strong and assertive Hindu nationalism would soon find disturbing expression.

F. SUMMARY

The disturbing prospects, however, return us to this book's theme, that of ferment. Much of this could be assessed very negatively, as did Valentine Chirol in *Indian Unrest*. Certainly

[25]Ibid., p. 157.

[26]Swami Vivekananda, *Collected Works*, vol. 3 (Calcutta: Advaita Ashrama, 1926), p. 242.

[27]Haridas and Uma Mukherjee, *Bipin Chandra Pal and India's Struggle for Swaraj* (Calcutta: Firm K. L. Mukhopadhyay, 1958), pp. 3—18.

[28]Donald E. Smith, *India as a Secular State* (Princeton: Princeton University Press, 1963), p. 90.

there had been excesses, and from the colonialist's reading of
history, those on the part of the people of India could, as in
1857, be viewed as mutinous. Alternately, it is easy to romanti-
cize indiscriminately on all fomenters of change if the ultimate
ends are viewed as valuable. Reform measures, strides toward
independence would be judged as positive achievements by
most viewers of the Indian scene, but critical historical perspectives must be employed in weighing various personal contributions to those goals.

Beyond the axiological questions, however, which can only
be alluded to here, another constant beyond that of ferment
serves to make more precise the character of the modern period
in India. R. C. Majumdar gives us an analogy for it when he
states that the chief personalities of nineteenth century India
may be likened to the shoots of a banyan tree, united in their
common root of spirituality.[29] The ferment that characterized
this period was religious in character; secularization was not
yet a viable stance, although a few persons such as Vidyasagar
at times anticipated it. The leaders who emerged, often at odds
with each other, couched their appeals in religious language
and were heard as spiritual persons. The profound question
remaining was whether this spirituality could translate into a
unitive, ethical ideal for the people of India.

[29]R. C. Majumdar, op. cit., p. 95.

by
Arvind Sharma

Introduction

Just as the year 1757 is often, somewhat arbitrarily, taken as marking the beginning of the British Period of Indian history, the year 1947 is seen as terminating it, perhaps with greater justification. With the same inevitability with which science must classify, history must periodize to gain coherence. But periods create the fiction of neat beginnings and ends; one tends to lose sight of the fact that moving from one period into another involves a rite of passage of sorts for a people. The impression of the occurrence of an overnight change so radical as the loss of virginity is misleading; often the preceding merges into the succeeding, and the succeeding emerges from the preceding. This is as true of the periods preceding and following the British as of any other.

It is difficult to write about a period so close to one's own. One is the product of that period and bears its stamp and scars. Moreover, the abundance of material in which the chronicler of the period might revel creates its own problems. Besides the danger that an embarrassment of evidentiary richness may paradoxically lead to a poverty of impartial analysis, one is forced to be selective and thus room is created for distortion to occur at the very inception. Perhaps the best one can do is to be conscious of the danger and try to overcome it. The claim to objectivity may turn out to a chimera of western self-assurance but the pursuit of impartiality is perhaps still laudable. In brief, an undertaking such as this must assume a considerable measure of benevolence on the part of the reader.

The first half of this century seems to have been characterized, in retrospect, by the consolidation of the major religious communities of the Indian subcontinent and by an effort to work out a *modus vivendi* among them. The final outcome is in the lap of the gods (or of God), but at least the process can be identified. Perhaps even this characterization is open to question, but if one stays with this view the various religious communities tend to represent sockets of sometimes shared and sometimes separate experience which the white heat of the great concentration of energy represented by the Independence Movement against the British could not weld into one shining chandelier of a Pan-Indian nationalism.

CHAPTER ONE

The British in India: New Patterns in an Established Relationship

On February 18, 1930 *The Times* brought out a Special India Number.[1] It is an interesting document if for no other reason than for the acknowledgement, even though in passing, that "The Congress Party is now committed to the ultimate goal of complete independence of India.[2] It also hastened to add, however, that in view "of the continued prevalence of communal and racial schisms . . . it is more than ever certain that British rule alone is the power which holds together all the diverse elements of a nation *in posse*."[3] The illusion of the permanence of British Raj[4] was still there but now had to be deliberately cultivated. The Introduction to the hard-cover reprint of the special India Number also expresses "a special and melancholy interest in the fact that these pages contain the last work of two distinguished contributors—Sir Valentine Chirol, who had written so much in *The Times* on Indian affairs, and Colonel Faunthorpe, the well-known *shikari* . . ." The juxtaposition of these two figures is not without interest. Colonel Faunthorpe seems to stand for the India that was passing away—the India of Sahibs and Shikars and cricket on Sundays. By contrast, Sir Valentine Chirol, in his writings, seemed to pre-figure the India that was emerging—an India restive under the British yoke.

---

[1]*India: A Reprint of The Special India Number of The Times February 18, 1930* (London: The Times Publishing Company Ltd, 1930).
[2]Ibid., p. 25.
[3]Ibid.
[4]see Francis G. Hutchins *The Illusion of Permanence* (Princeton University Press, 1967) passim.

India was no longer the unchanging static India. By the time first decade of the century was to end, it was to become fairly obvious that India was in transition though it may not have been quite clear what destination it was transiting to.

What had changed or was changing? And what had brought about this change?

A. THE ECONOMIC CONNECTION

The original incentive behind the British expansion in India, as well as of the European expansion over the globe, is generally believed to have been essentially mercantile in inspiration. Already during the eighteenth century, however, the British interest in India had gone far beyond being merely mercantile and had become colonial. It remained so firmly during the nineteenth century, although in a somewhat altered way. When the British took over effective control of Bengal after 1757, England had not yet had its industrial revolution. It has even been suggested that a rough parity may have existed in the standard of living and level of industrial development between India and England at the time. By 1900, however, the situation had altered radically. England was industrial, rich and prosperous; India was agricultural, poor and famine-ridden.

Not only had the relative levels of prosperity of India and England undergone a radical alteration, so had the nature of the relationship as a result of the industrial revolution in Britain. "As in Bengal, the decay of trade and industry in the rest of India set in towards the close of the eighteenth century and its ruin was well-nigh complete by the middle of the nineteenth."[5] During this time "the advent of new and cheap machine-made goods from the West gradually changed men's tastes and habits."[6] At the same time the first signs of industrialization in India began to appear,[7] a process which was accelerated by the First World War.

The poverty of India began to demand an explanation by

[5]R.C. Majumdar, H.C. Raychaudhuri, Kalikinkar Datta, *An Advanced History of India* (London: Macmillan, 1967) p. 804.
[6]Ibid., p. 894.
[7]Ibid., p. 895.

the turn of the nineteenth century and the unequal nature of the economic connection between India and England became one of the favourite Indian explanations of it. It was even claimed by Indian nationalists that the industrial revolution in Britain itself was "a consequence of the plundered wealth of India."[8] In any case, the unequal nature of the connection became a major Indian grievance against British rule, abetted by the Drain Theory.[9]

The economic condition of India in the early part of the twentieth century and the controversy surrounding it also had a religious context to it. The causes of the poverty of India gave rise to a debate which continues to rage,[10] a debate which has an important bearing on the study of Hinduism. Western scholars tended to account for this poverty largely in terms of Indian, and mainly Hindu attitudes[11] and institutions while Indian scholars tended to account for it in terms of British exploitation.[12] Thus one was left, in the end, with Hinduism and Imperialism as the two competing explanations of India's poverty, though semetimes both were cited as villains.[13]

B. IMPERIALISM

If, at the beginning of the nineteenth century, the philosophical justification of British Rule in India was provided by Utilitarianism, at the beginning of the twentieth century it was pro-

---

[8]Ibid., p. 805. Also see Robert I. Crane, ed., op. cit., p. 207-210.

[9]see Dadabhai Naoroji, *Poverty and un-British Rule in India* (Government of India, 1965 (first published 1901) passim; Birendranath Ganguli, *Dadabhai Naoroji and the Drain Theory* (Bombay: Asia Publishing House, 1965) passim.

[10]see Arvind Sharma, *The Hindu Scriptural Value System and the Economic Development of India* (New Delhi: Heritage Publishers, 1980) passim.

[11]see T. Parsons, ed., Max Weber, *The Protestant Ethic and Spirit of Capitalism* (New York: Charles Scribner's Sons, 1958) pp. 25-27; W.J. Kapp, *Hindu Culture, Economic Development and Economic Planning* New York: Asia Publishing House, 1963) passim.

[12] see R. Palme Dutt, *India Today* (London: Victor Gollancz, 1940) passim; etc.

[13]L.S.S. O'Malley, ed , *Modern India and the West* (London: Oxford University Press, 1941) p. 258.

vided by Imperialism. It is important to recognize in this connection that the situation is "not to be judged, perhaps, by Commandments recited west of Suez[14]". The conquest of India entailed the need to justify it and that justification was offered by people like Sir Alfred Lyall in terms of a lofty imperialism. He wrote in 1910: "At different times in the world's history the nations foremost in civilization have undertaken the enterprise of founding a great European dominion in Asia, and have accomplished it with signal success."[15] He then speaks of the Macedonian Greeks and the Romans whose Empires "have disappeared long ago, leaving very little but scattered ruins." Then he adds: "in modern times it is the British dominion in India that has revived and is pursuing the enterprise of ruling and civilizing a great Asiatic population, of developing the political intelligence and transforming the ideas of an antique, and, in some respects, a primitive society."[16] But after going on record in these terms, he remarks: "That the task must be one of prodigious difficulty, not always free from danger, has been long known to those who watched the experiment with some accurate foresight of the conditions attending it. Yet the recent symptoms of virulent disease in some parts of the body politic, though confined to certain provinces in India, have taken the British nation by surprise."[17]

This "virulent disease" was that of nationalism.[18] Sir Alfred C. Lyall was perhaps too close to the event to directly connect imperialism with nationalism though he does juxtapose the two. With the passage of time it is now possible to see the relationship between the two more clearly. The fact that

[14]Will Durant, *Our Oriental Heritage* (New York: Simon and Schuster, 1954) p. 614.

[15]Valentine Chirol, *Indian Unrest* (London: Macmillan & Co. Ltd, 1910) p. viii.

[16]Ibid.

[17]Ibid.

[18]see Anil Seal, *The Emergence of Indian Nationalism* (Cambridge University Press, 1968) passim. For a discussion of the various factors involved in its emergence see R. C. Majumdar, ed., *British Paramountcy and Indian Renaissance* Part II (Bombay: Bharatiya Vidya Bhavan, 1965) Chapter XIII.

nalionalism was regarded as "un-Indian"[19] and that India itself was not regarded as a nation may have delayed the recognition of the causal connection between imperialism and the rise of nationalism. After all, as late as 1972 a bemused Western news analyst remarked that "India is not even a geographical expression, but a rather muddled state of mind."[20]

Like the economic connection, the political connection between India and Britain too had led to the growth of nationalism.

C. EVANGELISM

Evangelical activity in India continued uninterrupted throughout the twentieth century but while "at the time of the Mutiny, there were many missionaries in India who sincerely believed that within a few generations the whole of India would become Christian,"[21] it was apparent by 1900 that this was unlikely. "The response of the great majority was simply a firm and uncompromising 'No'." This, however, should not lead one to the conclusion that Christian missionary activity made no impact in India. It may be useful here to distinguish between two aspects of the evangelical movement in evaluating its impact on India: (1) actual conversions to Christianity and (2) the impact of the Christian presence in India as a whole.

In terms of actual conversion "it seems that in 1914 the Christians in the whole of India numbered about three and a half million. Of these nearly two thirds were Roman Catholic, 10 per cent Christians of the independent Syrian churches, and about a quarter Protestant."[22] In 1930 the Christian community constituted 2 per cent of India's population. This community was unevenly distributed over the country. "In some areas of the south they were so numerous as to produce on the mind

[19]Percival Spear, *The Oxford History of Modern India 1740-1947* (Oxford: Clarendon Press, 1965) p. 289.

[20]quoted in Troy Wilson Organ, *Hinduism: Its Historical Development* (Woodbury, New York: Barron's Educational Series, Inc. 1974) p. 358.

[21]R.C. Zaehner, ed:, *The Concise Encyclopedia of Living Faiths* (Boston: Beacon Press, 1959) p. 259 .

[22]Stephen Neill, *The Story of the Christian Church in India and Pakistan* (Madras: 1972) p. 125-126.

of the visitor almost the impression of being in a Christian country", but in many areas they were a "tiny minority."[23] Most members of the Christian community in India were drawn from the lower classes. Another aspect of the Christian presence in India was that most of the missionaries, whose number greatly increased after 1858, were foreigners; and that as the years went by the proportion of women workers exceeded those of men.

The non-conversion of India to Christianity led many Christians to revise their position on the role of Christianity in India. This conversion was now seen as taking place over the long haul. It was to be the culmination of a process for which Hinduism itself prepared the people of India.[24] Whether this vision will be realized remains to be seen.

In terms of actual conversions, then, the evangelical movement was not a spectacular success but its impact on India went far beyond its numbers. "On the practical side it presented the Christian ethics in action and on the intellectual side it influenced by implication even more than by precept. Most missionaries presented the gospel in its western dress and they were therefore apostles of the West as well as of the pure spirit of Christ. By their manners and conduct, by their very existence, they were influences in favour of the western outlook. In these ways and in these respects Christian missionaries of all kinds exercised a profound influence, which can never be exactly measured, on the development of the new India. The influence was both positive and negative; negative by criticism of the old and positive by embodying the new ethic in personal example and corporate practice."[25]

It must be admitted, however, that though "Christianity has made its mark in India" it was "only at second hand."[26] Moreover, it played a major role in the religious ferment in India in the nineteenth century rather than the twentieth by which time nationalism, with a strong Hindu component, had

[23]Ibid., p, 126.

[24]see John Nicol Farquhar, *The Crown of Hinduism* (Delhi: Oriental books, 1971 [first published 1913]) passim.

[25]Percival Spear, op. cit., p. 280-281.

[26]R.C. Zaehner ed., op. cit, p. 259.

become a major force.

D. ORIENTALISM

It was noted earlier, in Chapter One of Part Two, how the work of Orientalists like Sir William Jones "came as a balm" "to a people who had sunk so low as the people of Bengal in the eighteenth century."[27] By the turn of the nineteenth century, however, the balm had become a tonic. As K. M. Panikkar has remarked:

The great work of Sir William Jones also began to bear unexpected fruit in India. The cultivation of Sanskrit in Europe opened the eyes of Indians to the great riches that their ancestors had left to them. It may sound strange but it is none the less true that it was the enthusiasm of Max Muller, Monier Williams and others for the culture of India that gave the first impetus to the modern study of classics in India. Also it was through the translations published by European scholars in English that the new middle classes began to know of the higher things in their own thought. The Sacred Books of the East published under the inspiration of Max Muller and the study of Indian philosophy in the West gave added impetus to the sense of nationalism that was daily growing in India.[28]

Thus, in a sense, the Orientalists were getting back at Macaulay in a rather unexpected way! This revivalism was aided by the participation of prominent Europeans. Valentine Chirol, who has been referred to earlier and who visited India in the first decade of the twentieth century, asks rhetorically, when speaking of Mrs Annie Beasant: "Is it surprising that Hindus should turn their backs upon our civilization when a European of highly trained intellectual power and with an extraordinary gift of eloquence comes and tells them that it is they who possess

[27]K.M. Panikkar, *A Survey of Indian History* (London: Meridian Books Ltd., 1947) p. 257.
[28]Ibid·, p. 268-269.

and have from all times possessed the key to supreme wisdom; that their gods, their philosophy, their morality are on a higher plane of thought than the West has ever reached?"[29]

Thus many of the aspects of the British presence in India in the eighteenth and nineteenth centuries continued into the twentieth—but with significant changes. The economic connection had become more industrial than commercial, the political philosophy had become clearly imperialistic, in religious outlook evangelical optimism was replaced by a sense of puzzlement at the resilience of Hinduism and the intellectual connection with its emphasis on western education was soon to lead to demand for western modes of government, while Orientalism had imparted a new cultural confidence to the people.

There was, however, also a new element in the situation, the product of the combined action of the many forces in operation discussed above. It was nationalism. It is this nationalism which was to distinguish the India of the twentieth century from the India of the nineteenth century. It came out of the religious closet, as it were, in the political arena in 1905 with the Partition of Bengal. And from then onwards the religious ferment in India can hardly be understood apart from the nationalist movement. "The progress of the nationalist movement forms the most important feature of Indian history during the first half of the present century."[30] This topic of nationalism deserves to be discussed in a separate chapter.

[29]Valentine Chirol, op. cit., p. 29.
[30]R.C. Majumdar et al., op. cit., p. 976.

| Nationalism and Religion in
Modern India

It may be useful, at the very outset, to distinguish between
political nationalism and religious nationalism. These two
streams of nationalism, though never entirely separated from
each other, are distinguishable from each other and provide
the warp and the woof out of which the destiny of modern
India was woven. To begin with, they seem to have been
relatively independent. The major spokesmen of the Hindu
renaissance in the nineteenth century, people like Swami
Dayananda[1] and Swami Vivekananda[2] by and large stayed
away from "politics". This was not to be the case later, at
least to the same extent, as when Mahatma Gandhi was to
write: "Those who say that religion has nothing to do with
politics do not know what religion means."[3]

The first formal forum where the stirrings of political
nationalism found their expression was the Indian National
Congress, founded in Bombay in December 1885.[4] This political
movement, which had now found an institutional expression,
may be seen as passing through four distinct, though connected,
phases from the point of view of our concerns.

(1) The first phase may be said to extend from 1885-1905.

[1]see J.T.F. Jordens, *Dayananda Sarasvati, His Life and Ideas* (Delhi:
Oxford University Press, 1978) passim.

[2]E.F. Malcolm-Smith (tr.) Romain Rolland, *The Life of Vivekananda*
(Calcutta: Advaita Ashrama, 1965) p. 115, 135.

[3]Mahadev Desai (tr.) M.K. Gandhi, *An Autobiography* (London:
Jonathan Cape, 1972 [first published 1972]) p. 420,

[4]Percival Spear, op. cit., p. 293.

During this phase the Indian National Congress basically represented democratic liberalism and the movement of religious nationalism, if anything, was somewhat opposed to it.[5]

(2) The second phase may be said to extend from 1905-1920. During this phase "the Congress nationalist movement was frankly Hindu and revivalist."[6]

(3) The third phase may be said to extend from 1920-1940 when the Congress represented the "resistance of India as a whole to alien domination" and "the political purpose of the Congress and its general outlook in regard to the future of India was entirely non-sectarian."[7]

(4) The fourth phase may be seen as extending from 1940-1947, during which the two major religious components of Indian nationalism—the Hindu and the Muslim—jointly or singly led to the political bifurcation of the country.

The period also witnessed the successful achievement of the major goal of political nationalism, namely, political independence.

A. FIRST PHASE

There are at least three pieces of evidence which go to show that political nationalism, as expressed through the Indian National Congress from 1885—1905, was largely independent of religious nationalism. The first of these is the fact that during this period "there was a renaissance of Hinduism, which was inspired by *reaction against western influences*"[8] while the members of the Congress, at this time, "represented a Western and liberal point of view and were great admirers of the British."[9] The renaissance of Hinduism referred to above is an allusion to the fact that during this period "Three distinct religious movements sprang up: viz. the Arya Samaj in North India, which was founded by Dayanand Saraswati in 1875,

---

[5]L.S.S, O'Malley, ed., op. cit., p. 90-91.
[6]K.M. Panikkar, op. cit., p. 274.
[7]Ibid., p. 276.
[8]L.S.S. O'Malley, ed., op. cit., p. 91.
[9]K.M. Panikkar, op. cit., p. 273.

the Ramakrishna Mission in Bengal, which was started in 1897 by the disciples of Ramakrishna Paramhamsa under the leadership of Swami Vivekananda, and the Theosophical Society in South India."[10]

The second piece of evidence which shows the relative independence of the political nationalism as expressed through the Indian National Congress from the religious, while at the same time illustrating how thin was the line which separated them, is the fact that when in 1887 "a Hindu delegate wished to move a resolution in favour of prohibition of cow-killing, which the Muslims would have opposed tooth and nail. . .it had to be laid down that no resolution should be moved, and no subject discussed, to which there was unanimous or nearly unanimous objection on the part of either the Hindu or Muslim delegates."[11] Thirdly, it may be noted that Muslim nationalism, as represented by Sir Sayyid Ahmad Khan, opposed the "Congress movement as a Hindu one."[12]

It is obvious, then, that at this stage in the evolution of political nationalism it was kept more or less insulated from religious nationalism and to a certain extent was suspect in the eyes of Hindu and Muslim nationalists. Not only did the Muslim community by and large take "no part in the movement, but resolved to abstain from political agitation, under the leadership of Sir Sayyid Ahmad Khan, who founded an anti-Congress association," the "Congress also failed to obtain support from the great body of Hindu conservative opinion."[13]

B. SECOND PHASE

The situation changed dramatically with the Partition of Bengal in 1905. The agitation against the Partition of Bengal both extended the popular base of political nationalism and also gave to it a Hindu character. An interesting account of both these developments as manifesting themselves in the life of an Indian can be found in Chapter III of the autobiography of

[10]L.S.S. O'Malley, op. cit., p. 91.
[11]Ibid., p. 747.
[12]Ibid.
[13]L.S.S. O'Malley, op. cit., p. 90.

"the brilliant, if sometimes eccentric," Bengali scholar Nirad Chaudhuri.[14] More generally, the political significance of the agitation against the Partition of Bengal lay in the fact that ultimately "the issue, until then successfully veiled and now openly raised, was not whether Bengal should be one unpartitioned province or two partitioned provinces under British rule, but whether British rule itself was to endure in Bengal or, for that matter, anywhere in India."[15] Moreover, the agitation against the British also acquired an economic dimension through the boycott of British goods under the slogan of *Swadeshi*. It also led to the "growth of a radical section in the Congress" and increase in terrorist activity against the British. The agitation against the Partition of Bengal resulted in a "general state of serious unrest" not just in Bengal but even in the Punjab and Madras.[16]

In order to popularize the agitation the leaders of the agitation appealed to Hindu symbols and sentiments. Thus even Surendranath Banerjee "urged that a religious turn be given to the movement by means of ceremonies in honor of Kali and Sakti, and meetings held in temples and vows to boycott British goods taken in the name of Kali did much to popularize the cause."[17]

It was mentioned earlier that one consequence of this agitation was to strengthen the radical wing within the Congress. The Congress, when it met in 1906, "for the first time in its history, laid down as its goal 'the system of government obtaining in the self-governing British colonies', which the President summed up in one word, 'Swarāj'."[18] The chief spokesmen of this new spirit were B. G. Tilak, B. C. Pal and Lajpat Rai, who belonged to the so-called "extremist" section. It clashed with the "moderates" represented by S. N. Banerjee, P. S. Mehta and B. G. Gokhale in 1907 at Surat and stayed out of the

[14]reproduced in Thomas R. Metcalf, ed., *Modern India: An Interpretive Anthology* (London: The Macmillan Company, 1971) Chapter 16.

[15]Valentine Chirol, op. cit., p. 88.

[16]R.C. Majumdar, et al, op. cit., p. 924.

[17]L.S.S. O'Malley, op. cit., p. 751. For a more detailed account of the interaction of political and religious nationalism in this case see Valentine Chirol, op. cit., Chapter VII.

[18]R.C. Majumdar et al, op. cit., p. 977.

Congress for nine years, uniting with them in 1916 at Lucknow.

It was shown earlier how Surendranath Banerjee, a "moderate", advocated the use of religious sentiment and symbolism to serve political ends. This applies with more force to the extremist leaders Balgangadhar Tilak, B.C. Pal and Lala Lajpat Rai—the BAL-PAL-LAL triumvirate to which mention has already been made in Chapter Seven of Part One.

C. THIRD PHASE

The next major phase is represented by the emergence of Mahatma Gandhi as the leader of the Congress. By the end of the second decade of the century, several factors had contributed to the growth of political nationalism "two of which deserve special mention, viz. the atrocities in the Punjab and the Khilafat agitation."[19] In 1919 the Government introduced a set of repressive measures known as the Rowlatt Acts to suppress political nationalism and this resulted in what is known as the Amritsar massacre,[20] in which the army fired on an unarmed crowd. "The casualties were officially estimated at 379 killed and over 200 wounded. This was followed by the proclamation of martial law, severe punitive measures, and humiliating orders. Order was restored in the Panjab but a scar was drawn across Indo-British relations deeper than any which had been inflicted since the Mutiny. Racial feeling was intense."[21] While on the one hand opposition to the British intensified, the movement against the British also became unified. The Muslims resented the part played by the British in the dismemberment of the Turkish Empire and a movement against the British was organized by the Ali brothers. Mahatma Gandhi and the Congress supported this movement wholeheartedly which resulted in "unprecedented fraternisation between the Hindus and the Muslims."

Thus by 1920 Mahatma Gandhi had emerged as the leader of the Congress. The crucial issue henceforth was to be whether

[19]R.C. Majumdar et al, op. cit., p. 980.

[20]see R.C. Majumdar, ed., *Struggle for Freedom* (Bombay: Bharatiya Vidya Bhavan, 1969) Chapter XI.

[21]Percival Spear, op. cit., p. 341.

political nationalism in India was strong enough to dislodge the British and broad enough to absorb religious nationalisms—which found expression during this period in the activities of the Hindu Mahasabha among the Hindus and the All-India Muslim League among the Muslims. With the benefit of hindsight K.M. Panikkar has remarked that "The period of co-operation with the Muslim League and the interlude of the Khilafat agitation should not blind us to the fact that the strength of the Congress lay primarily in the Hindu revival and in an integral nationalism based on the Hindu masses."[22] This Hindu component of Mahatma Gandhi's appeal is thus identified by L.S.S. O'Malley:

> The secret of Mr. Gandhi's success in the political education of the masses lay in the fact that not only was he invested with the halo of a saint in popular estimation, but that he brought them a message which, while arousing a nationalist feeling, gave life to spiritual aspirations. Religious and moral teachings, true to Hindu ideals, went hand in hand with political propaganda, and nationalism was presented in a religious garb. He struck a note which vibrated in the hearts of Hindus by declaring that the *Rama Raj* would return. This is the golden age of Hinduism, on which Hindus wistfully look back, an age of peace, prosperity, and happiness, in which every family had an ample holding of land and enjoyed the fruits of its labour without the incubus of rent. At the same time he urged his hearers and readers to learn the art and beauty of self-denial and simplicity of life; and the simple garb of homespun cloth worn by himself and his followers, rich as well as poor, was not without its psychological effect. The form of agitation which he prescribed was passive resistance, a traditional means of opposition to government in India, which was variously called non-violent non-co-operation or civil disobedience.[23]

It is a much debated point in modern Indian history whether the Hindu colouration of political nationalism is to be blamed for

[22] K.M. Panikkar, op. cit., p. 276.
[23] L.S.S. O'Malley, ed., op. cit., p. 97—98.

the alienation of the Muslims[24] or the divide-and-rule tactics of the British[25] or perhaps both. It cannot be gainsaid, however, that by 1940 the Muslims of India felt sufficiently alienated to demand an independent Muslim state[26] in the event of a British withdrawal. The turning-point in the Muslim attitude is said to be the Congress decision in 1937 not to form a Coalition ministry with the Muslim League after sweeping the polls in elections held under the Government of India Act of 1935 under which a measure of self-government was introduced in India.[27] If, however, this assertion is substantially true then it is of capital significance in the history of the interaction between political and religious nationalism. For here we have a case where a *political* decision may have had religious implications of the first magnitude. The above-mentioned political decision, if it was the proximate cause for the formation of Pakistan, ultimately not only intensified the religious ferment in India but may have led to a religious crisis—resulting in the convulsions which accounted for and then followed the formation of Pakistan. What has been referred to as the "second phase" above also seems to present an example of a similar development. If the Partition of Bengal, a political or administrative act, did much to inflame feelings against the British and laid the foundations of the Hindu-Muslim divide in Indian politics[28] then here we once again have an illustration of a decision taken in the political arena producing reactions both in the areas of political as well as religious nationalism. The influence of religion on politics is often pointed out but the influence of politics on religion, it seems, may have been equally consequential in the context of religious ferment in modern India.

[24]see Choudhry Khaliquzzaman, *Pathway to Pakistan* (Lahore: Longmans, 1961) passim.

[25]Robert I. Crane, ed., op. cit., p. 303.

[26]For the deeper roots of this see Hafeez Malik, *Moslem Nationalism in India and Pakistan* (Washington: Public Affairs Press, 1963).

[27]R.C. Majumdar et al, op. cit., p. 19: Wm. Theodore de Bary, ed., *Sources of Indian Tradition* Vol. II (New York: Columbia University Press, 1958) p. 282.

[28]D.A. Low, ed., *Soundings in Modern South Asian History* (Canberra: Australian National University Press, 1968) Chapter 7.

D. Fourth Phase

Thus the fourth phase of the interaction between political and religious nationalism witnessed the centripetal forces of political nationalism being overcome by the centrifugal forces of religious nationalism seeking political expression. Already by 1930 the signs of the parting of ways between Indian and Muslim nationalism were beginning to surface and by 1947 Pakistan had become a reality.[29] It has been said that "Sayyid Ahmad Khan gave Indian Islam a sense of separate existence; Iqbal a sense of separate destiny"[30] and that "The ideology of Iqbal, the visions of Rahmat Ali, and the fears of Muslims...were united by the practical genius of Jinnah to bind Muslims together as never before during the British period and lead (*sic*) to effect an act of political creation."[31]

One interesting aspect of the interaction between political and religious nationalism is the fact that the spokesmen of both Hinduism and Islam held different views regarding the relationship between the two, apart from the fact that some of them, especially those on the Islamic side, also held different views about them at different stages of their life. Thus the "Ali brothers swung round from the preaching of Hindu fraternalism to the championship of Muslim rights."[32] Iqbal became convinced of the futility of Hindu-Muslim unity towards the end of life[33] and "Mr. Jinnah, who later propounded the theory that Hindus and Muslims represent two separate nations "had once vehemently protested against the view that India was not a nation."[34]

From the point of view of this relationship of religious and

---

[29]"An Indian Muslim student at Cambridge, Chaudhari Rahmat Ali, coined the word Pakistan, by taking P from Punjab, A from Afghania (by which name he preferred to call the North-Western Frontier Province), K for Kashmir, S for Sind, and *Tan* for Baluchis-tan. The I between K and S does not occur if the name is written in Urdu. The synthetic name also had a meaning—the Land of the Pure." (Wm. Theodore de Bary, ed., op. cit., p. 275).

[30]Percival Spear, op. cit., p. 362.

[31]Ibid., p. 363.

[32]Ibid.

[33]Wm. Theodore de Bary ed., op. cit., p. 199.

[34]R.C. Majumdar et al, op. cit., p. 985.

political nationalism it might be useful to "consider three outstanding Hindus of the twentieth century who have held differing opinions of the relation of Hinduism and nationalism: Rabindranath Tagore, Aurobindo Ghose, and Mahatma Gandhi.[35] Once this is done, their understanding of Hinduism itself could be commented upon, as affected by the religious ferment in modern India.

[35]Troy Wilson Organ, op. cit., p. 358.

| Rabindranath Tagore

Rabindranath Tagore (1861-1941) was one of the key figures of modern India. He was described by Will Durant as "perhaps the most impressive of all men now on the earth,"[1] a tribute evocative of Einstein's tribute to Mahatma Gandhi. Indeed "The landmarks of his life," like those of Mahatma Gandhi, "have already passed into history—his life on the Padma river in East Bengal, where he assimilated the folk traditions in Indian culture; his role in the Swadeshi movement; the award of the Nobel Prize for literature and the author's world-wide fame; association with Mahatma Gandhi; the establishment of the school at Shantiniketan, and later the international university (*Vishwabharati*); travels in South East Asia and the Far East; lectures in Europe and America; meetings with leading statesmen, thinkers, artists and poets of the contemporary world; indictment of Imperialism and Fascism. Though a familiarity with these events is important for a complete understanding of Tagore's personality and work, our main concern here is with his *thought*,"[2] especially as arising out of and contributing to the religious ferment in modern India.

Rabindranath Tagore, who has sometimes been compared

[1]Will Durant, op. cit., p 621.

[2]V.S. Naravane, *Modern Indian Thought* (New Delhi : Orient Longmans, 1978) p. 110. For more on his life see Krishna Kriplani, *Rabindranath Tagore A Biography* (London : Oxford University Press 1962).

to Goethe, was a man of many parts — poet, artist and prophet.[3]
Here, we are concerned primarily with his views on the relation
between nationalism and Hinduism and then about Hinduism
itself.

A. TAGORE AND NATIONALISM

Rabindranath Tagore took a dim view of nationalism. He
regarded nationalism as a disease of the West claiming that "we
have no word for 'Nation' in our language. When we borrow
this word from other people, it never fits us."[4] This contrast
between the East and the West on this point is brought out
clearly in the poem "The Sunset of the Century" written on the
occasion of the Boer War, "on the last day of the last
century."[5]

1

The last sun of the century sets amidst the blood-red
    clouds of the West and the whirlwind of hatred.
The naked passion of self-love of Nations, in its
    drunken delirium of greed, is dancing to the clash
    of steel and the howling verses of vengeance.

2

The hungry self of the Nation shall burst in a violence
    of fury from its own shameless feeding.
For it has made the world its food.
And licking it, crunching it, and swallowing it in big
    morsels.
It swells and swells,
Till in the midst of its unholy feast descends the
    sudden shaft of heaven piercing its heart of
    grossness.

[3]D.S. Sarma, *Studies in the Renaissance of Hinduism* (Benaras
Hindu University, 1944) p. 340-343. On his versatility see *Rabindranath
Tagore 1861-1961 A Centenary Volume* (New Delhi: Sahitya Akademi,
1961).

[4]quoted in Troy Wilson Organ, op. cit., p. 359.

[5]Krishna Kripalani, op. cit., p. 183.

3

The crimson glow of light on the horizon is not the
light of thy dawn of peace, my Motherland.
It is the glimmer of the funeral pyre burning to ashes
the vast flesh—the self-love of the Nation—dead
under its own excess.
Thy morning waits behind the patient dark of the East,
Meek and silent.

4

Keep watch, India.
Bring your offerings of worship for that sacred sunrise.
Let the first hymn of its welcome sound in your voice
and sing
"Come, Peace, thou daughter of God's own great
suffering.
Come with thy treasure of contentment, the sword of
fortitude.
And meekness crowning thy forehead."

5

Be not ashamed, my brothers, to stand before the
proud and the powerful.
With your white robe of simpleness.
Let your crown be of humility, your freedom the
freedom of the soul.
Build God's throne daily upon the ample bareness of
your poverty
And know that what is huge is not great and pride is
not everlasting.[6]

It would, however, be a mistake to conclude from this that
Tagore was a West-hater or a West-baiter. He denounced not
only Western nationalism but nationalism per se as well.[7] Even
when he denounced Western nationalism,[8] he drew a radical
distinction between what he called "the spirit of the West" as

---

[6]Wm. Theodore de Bary, ed., op. cit., p. 234-235.
[7]Troy Wilson Organ, op. cit., p. 360.
[8]see Wm. Theodore de Bary, op. cit., p. 236-238; D. S. Sarma,
op. cit., p. 344.

opposed to "the Nation of the West."[9] He denounced the latter
but extolled the former. "By 'the spirit of the West' Tagore
meant the active productivity, the energetic mode of life characteristic of the West, by 'the nation of the West' he meant the
entire apparatus of government which stresses equality and
uniformity."[10]

Whenever Tagore thought that India was becoming infected
with the virus of nationalism he protested strongly, if uneffecti-
vely. Thus he "entered into a controversy with Bankim Chandra
Chatterjee over the neo-Hindu movement"[11] and after initially
participating in the agitation against the Partition of Bengal in
1905 "suddenly withdrew from the political field to the annoy-
ance of many of his countrymen and retired to Santiniketana."[12]

The crux of the matter is that Tagore was a champion of
humanism. This basic fact explains not only his condemnation
of nationalism and imperialism[13] but also the fluctuations in his
relationship with Mahatma Gandhi and his attitudes towards
Hinduism. His relationship with Mahatma Gandhi may be
briefly recounted:

For whatever reasons, Tagore and Gāndhi certainly disagreed
fundamentally in their diagnoses of India's ills and their
prescription for her cure. For a time this disagreement
clouded their personal friendship, which had dated from 1915
when Tagore had invited Gāndhi, fresh from South Africa,
to bring his followers to Shāntiniketan for want of a more
congenial temporary haven. Addressing Gāndhi on this
occasion as Mahātmā (great soul), Tagore seems to have been
the first to use the famous title. Their public controversy
over the methods of Gāndhi's noncooperation movement
flared up in 1921. . . .Gāndhi's 1933 fast against untouchability brought about a dramatic reconciliation between the two
men, and Gāndhi ended his fast with a sip of fruit juice while
Tagore sat nearby. Visiting Shāntiniketan after the poet's
death, Gāndhi is said to have remarked that he had begun by

[9]Ibid., p. 236; Troy Wilson Organ, op. cit., p. 360;
[10]Ibid.
[11]D.S. Sarma, op. cit., p. 358, 365.
[12]Ibid., p. 370; also see p. 365—366.
[13]Ibid , p. 378.

thinking that he and Tagore were poles apart, but now believed that in fundamentals they were one.[14]

Thus Mahatma Gandhi won Tagore's admiration for his opposition to racialism in South Africa but earned his censure when he seemed to be succumbing to nationalism. However, his fight against untouchability again won Tagore's admiration. Similarly, Tagore was critical of Hinduism whenever it ran counter to his humanist instincts. Thus he "had the courage to denounce the most basic of India's institutions—the caste system—and the dearest of her beliefs—transmigration,"[15] presumably because the latter provided the underpinning of the former. But he also thought "that Hinduism was a form of self-realization which rested upon the freedom of the individual to express himself in accord with the leanings of his own nature, and he feared that nationalism is destructive of the self. The nation, he believed, is a slave-producing institution which will in time drag human individuals to destruction. Therefore he saw Hinduism and nationalism as diametrically opposed; the former stresses the moral greatness of man, and the latter turns men into means for the glorification of the state. Tagore, reflecting upon his childhood, wrote, 'Even though from childhood I had been taught that idolatry of the nation is almost better than reverence for God and humanity, I believe I have outgrown that teaching, and it is my conviction that my countrymen will truly gain their India by fighting against the education which teaches them that a country is greater than the ideals of humanity.' "[16]

Hence the paradox that while a poem written by Rabindranath Tagore should be a national anthem of Independent India,[17] the ideal he espouses for his own country should be so sublime as to be universal.

> Where the mind is without fear and the head is held
> high;

[14]Wm. Theodore de Bary ed., op., cit., p. 230—231; also see V. S. Naravane, op. cit., p. 105-107.

[15]Will Durant, op. cit., p. 621; but see S. Radhakrishnan, *The Philosophy of Rabindranath Tagore* (London: Macmillan and Co., 1918) p. 63.

[16]Troy Wilson Organ, op. cit., p. 359.

[17]Wm. Theodore de Bary, ed., op. cit., p. 235-236.

> Where knowledge is free;
> Where the world has not been broken up into frag-
>   ments by narrow domestic walls;
> Where words come out from the depth of truth;
> Where tireless striving stretches its arms towards
>   perfection;
> Where the clear stream of reason has not lost its way
>   into the dreary desert sand of dead habit;
> Where the mind is ledforward by thee into everwiden-
>   ing thought and action—
> Into that heaven of freedom, my Father, let my
>   country awake.[18]

B. Tagore and Hinduism

The religious thought of Tagore is shot through with humanism
as the title of his work *The Religion of Man*[19] serves to remind
us. He espouses a theistic view of the ultimate reality, prefering
it to the Advaitic,[20] thereby creating more metaphysical room
for the celebration of humanism. This naturally leads the poet
in the direction of devotional mysticism[21] but here again he
departs from the tradition of the medieval devotional poets of
India, to whom he is heir, in two significant respects. Firstly,
Tagore "dispenses with all mythological symbols and sectarian
names and forms. He uses the universal language of man.[22] He

----

[18]Ibid., p. 236.

[19]Rabindranath Tagore, *The Religion of Man* (London: Allen and
Unwin, 1931).

[20]D. S. Sarma, op. cit., p. 386.

[21]Ibid., p. 388.

[22]Consider, for example, the following lines:

> I run as a musk-deer runs in the shadow of the forest mad
> with his own perfume.
> The night is the night of mid-May, the breeze is the breeze of
> the south.
> I lose my way and I wander, I seek what I cannot get, I get
> what I do not seek.
>
> From my heart comes out and dances the image of my own
> desire.
> The gleaming vision flits on.
> I try to clasp it firmly, it eludes me and leads me astray.

speaks of God as king, master, friend, father, poet, bridegroom
or lover, and not as any mythological deity or Avatār."[23]
Thus he is as human in outlook as he may be said to be
Hindu. Secondly, Tagore's poetry is life-affirming and not
tinged with ochre as was the case with the poetry of many
medieval religious poets.

> No, my friends. I shall never be an ascetic, whatever
>   you may say.
> I shall never be an ascetic if she does not take the
>   vow with me.
> It is my firm resolve that if I cannot find a shady
>   shelter and a companion for my penance, I shall
>   never turn ascetic.
>
> No, my friends, I shall never leave my hearth and
>   home, and retire into the forest solitude, if rings no
>   merry laughter in its echoing shade and if the end
>   of no saffron mantle flutters in the wind; if its silence
>   is not deepened by soft whispers.
> I shall never be an ascetic.[24]

But Tagore's religious sentiment is characterized as much by
Nature mysticism as by devotional mysticism. Indeed, as D. S.
Sarma has pointed out, "his originality consists not in his
poems of devotional mysticism, exquisite flowers of the heart
as they are, but in those of Nature mysticism. Here he breaks
what is practally new ground in our religious literature. For
in modern times we have had no conspicuous instances of
intense religious feeling arising out of love of Nature. It is
rather strange that in a country, where the Vedas themselves
arose out of a passionate feeling for the glories of Nature, this
type of poetry should have receded into the background. Even
the great Kālidāsa, with all his intense love and accurate

I seek what I cannot get, I get what I no not seek.
(Rabindranath Tagore, *The Gardner* [London: Macmillan &
Co., 1917] p. 35.)
[23]D. S. Sarma, op. cit., p. 388
[24]Rabindranath Tagore, *The Gardner*, p. 78.

knowledge of mountains, trees and flowers, had no *religious* feeling for Nature."[25]

Anticipations of Nature mysticism can be found in the Upanisads and the Bhagavadgītā[26] but it is in Tagore that it finds its finest expression. Several poems could be cited to illustrate this point; but it may be more worthwhile to indicate the religious emotion in which they have their source. It is revealed by the poet himself in a letter dated 20th August 1892:

I feel as if dim, distant memories come to me of the time when I was one with the rest of the earth; when on me grew green grass and on me fell the autumn light; when a warm scent of youth would rise from every pore of my vast, soft, green body at the touch of the rays of the mellow sun, and a fresh life, a sweet joy would be half-consciously secreted and inarticulately poured forth from all the immensity of my being. . .My feelings seem to be those of the ancient earth in the daily ecstasy of its sun-kissed life; my own consciousness seems to stream through each blade of grass, each sucking root, to rise with the sap through the trees, to break out with joyous thrills in the waving fields of corn, in the rustling palm-leaves.[27]

Thus Tagore's religious sentiment is characterized by a broad humanism, a universal if intense devotionalism and a spiritual naturism. The fact that it is so characterized served to bring into sharper focus and further enlarge these aspects of Hinduism.

C. Tagore's Influence

Before moving on to the next chapter it may be useful to "mark out the main determinants of his thought." V.S. Naravane identifies these determinants in the case of Tagore as follows:

(1) the Upanisads;

(2) the theistic-humanistic tradition as developed by (a) the

[25]D. S. Sarma, op. cit., p. 396.
[26]Ibid., p. 396-398.
[27]cited by D. S. Sarma, op. cit., p. 300-401.

Vaisnava poet-saints of medieval India and (b) the Bauls;

(3) Buddhism;

(4) the influence of European thought, literature and life-style.[28]

One must also, when dealing with the "sources of Tagore's thought" refer to " 'three upheavals' which, in his own judgement, influenced him considerably : the revolution in religion, initiated by Ram Mohun Roy, which 'led to the reopening of the channels of spiritual life'; 'the literary revolution, led by Bankim Chandra Chatterji, which liberated literature from the dead weight of convention and made it a living vehicle of experience; and the sociopolitical revolution which created a new faith in India's heritage and helped the Indian mind to redefine its notions in terms of modern ideas of freedom, equality and social justice'."[29]

A little reflection will show that these factors influenced not just Tagore but almost all the major thinkers of modern India in varying degrees. The life and thought of Sri Aurobindo illustrates this well.

[28]V. S. Naravane, *op. cit.*, p. 111-114.
[29]Ibid., p. 115.

CHAPTER FOUR | Aurobindo Ghosh

One of the characteristic features of the religious ferment in modern India was the "interaction between traditional Hindu religious life and Western intellectual traditions"[1] through the nineteenth and the twentieth centuries. It has been suggested that "Mohandas K. Gandhi (1869-1948) and Aurobindo Ghosh (1872-1950) are perhaps the best known and most influential representatives of this pattern in the twentieth century."[2] There is a greater measure of unanimity about the influential impact of Gandhi's work than that of Aurobindo, who sometimes leaves the "impression of being a little cut off from the Indian thought."[3] Interest in Aurobindo, however, seems to be on the increase, perhaps because he had set out to "create a new synthesis of truth by drawing upon both Hindu and Western thought in such a way that an original theological and philosophical construct would emerge. In engaging in this task he was attempting to do for the modern world what Shankarāchārya had done for Hinduism in the ninth century and St. Thomas Aquinas for Christianity in the thirteenth, but it is impossible to say how successful he has been"[4]—as yet.

[1]Thomas J. Hopkins, *The Hindu Religious Tradition* (Belmont, California : Dickenson Publishing Company, Inc., 1971) p. 137,

[2]Ibid., p. 138.

[3]V. S. Naravane, op. cit., p. 193.

[4]Ainslie T. Embree, ed., *The Hindu Tradition* (New York: Vintage Books, 1972) p. 328-329.

A. LIFE

Aurobindo's life is of some interest in itself as representing the interaction between India and the West and falls more or less clearly into three distinct phases. The first of these extends from his birth in 1872 to his return to India in 1893. At the age of seven, the young Aurobindo was sent to England by his Anglophile father to insulate him from Indian influences and he remained there till his twenty-first year. His father's hopes were fulfilled to the extent that Aurobindo became well-versed in Western learning but if his intention was to turn his son's thoughts away from India he failed. On the contrary, this prolonged absence may have had the effect of intensifying his love for India.[5]

The second phase of his life commenced with his return to India and may be said to end with his retirement from political life. Thus it covers the period extending from 1893-1910. In the first part of this period he was in the service of the Gaekwar of Baroda. During this period he 'Indianized' himself. Then in 1906, "Despite the fact that he was unusually shy, during the agitation against the Partition of Bengal he gave up his post as vice-principle of Baroda College and threw himself in the maelstrom of Bengal politics."[6] This participation ultimately led to his incarceration. During the period of detention in the Alipur jail "he had a profound religious experience, which totally altered the course of his life. He has vividly described it for us in his Uttarapara speech. He tells us how one day he saw in a vision the spirit of God all around him in the prison compound and, later, again in the court and heard a definite message. It came to him with the familiar form of the Bhagavan of the Gītā, whom he saw everywhere in place of the prison bars, the trees in compound, the prisoners in chains and, later, in place of the judge and counsel, while he stood in the dock. And a voice told him that he was being prepared for an altogether different kind of work which he should undertake after his release. The message said: 'Something has been shown to you in this year of seclusion, something about which you had your doubts and it is the truth of the Hindu religion. It is this

---

[5]Wm. Theodore de Bary, op. cit., p. 174.
[6]Ibid., p. 173.

religion that I am raising up before the world, it is this that I have perfected and developed through the ṛṣis, saints and avatārs, and now it is going forth to do my work among the nations. I am raising up this nation to send forth my word. This is the Sanātana Dharma, this is the eternal religion which you did not really know before, but which I have now revealed to you. The agnostic and the sceptic in you have been answered, for I have given you proofs within and without you, physical and subjective, which have satisfied you. When you go forth, speak to your nation always this word, that it is for the Sanātana Dharma that they arise, it is for the world and not for themselves that they arise. I am giving them freedom for the service of the world .... It is for the Dharma that India exists."[7]

Thus Aurobindo entered the third phase of his life. He left Bengal and repaired to Pondicherry in the South, then a French enclave in British India. He remained there till he died in 1950. His *magnum opus*, The Life Divine was written during this period of self-imposed exile, first appearing serially in the journal Ārya started by him.

B. AUROBINDO AND NATIONALISM

Initially it was not Aurobindo's spiritualism but his nationalism which made him a famous figure in India. This imparts a particular fascination to the study of the interaction of political and religious nationalism in Aurobindo. On one view the two got fused in him as nowhere else. Thus it has been said:

Brief as his political career was, Aurobindo defined the essence of religious nationalism in a manner which for sheer passion has never been surpassed. Because of his prolonged absence from India, Aurobindo came to idealize both his native land and its ancestral faith and to identify one with

[7]D. S. Sarma, op. cit., p. 311.

[8]For more details on some aspects of his life see Jan Feys, *The Life of a Yogi* (Calcutta: Firma K. L. Mukhopadhyay. 1976). Also see Robert N. Minor, *Sri Aurobindo: The Perfect and the Good* (Calcutta: Minerva Associates Pvt. Ltd, 1978).

the other in a way no previous thinker had dared to do. The
very fervor of his faith in "India" helped his Hindu countrymen to transcend the many differences of caste, language,
and customs which had hindered the development among
them of allegiance to one nation.

Aurobindo was free of the region-centered nationalism
which limited the effectiveness of a Bengali like Bankim or a
Mahārāshtrian like Tilak. Along with Bankim and Tilak,
however, he failed to perceive that the greater the zeal of the
   Hindu nationalists became, the more difficult grew the task
of uniting both Hindus and Muslims in loyalty to a single
non-British government.[9]

Troy Wilson Organ has, however, argued that although at
the time of his participation in the agitation sparked by the
Partition of Bengal he "displayed the narrow zeal characteristic
of a new convert," "even in these years of his youthful enthusi-
asms" there was this "redeeming feature of Aurobindo's
nationalism" that "India's existence as a free nation was not for
India's sake alone, but for the world."[10] "The liberation India
sought was not India's liberation but the liberation of mankind.
He retired to Pondicherry to spend the rest of his life working
out the implications of the larger liberation."[11] It is perhaps
of more than a little interest that "Aurobindo, like Tagore appeared to have doubts about the nationalism of India as he watched
the progress of the independence movement. He also feared
that India might imitate the West in structure and miss the
spirit . . . ."[12] Again, in his Independence Day Declaration he
emphasized that "international forms and institutions must
appear; perhaps such developments as dual and multilateral
citizenship, willed interchange of voluntary fusion of cultures."[13]

    [9]Ibid., p. 174. Also see David L. Johnson, *The Religious Roots of
Indian Nationalism: Aurobindo's early political thought* (Calcutta: Firma
K. L. Mukhopadhyay, 1974); Karan Singh, *Prophet of Indian National-
ism: a study of the political thought of Sri Aurobindo Ghosh 1893-1910*
London: Allen & Unwin, 1963).
    [10]Troy Wilson Organ, op. cit., p. 361-362.
    [11]Ibid., p. 362.
    [12]Ibid.
    [13]Ibid.

Thus there seems a good case for maintaining that "the nationalism of Aurobindo, like the nationalism of Tagore, turned into
an internationalism."[14] In the end, it seems, Aurobindo's religious nationalism became less national and more religious in
content.

C. AUROBINDO AND HINDU THOUGHT

There could be several ways of assessing Aurobindo's contribution to Hindu thought in the twentieth century.[15] One possible
way of determining his contributions could be to examine the
way in which he has tried to integrate what are typically Western intellectual categories with traditional Hindu thought. It
is this approach which will be adopted here. It may be useful
to look at four such categories and their use by Aurobindo:
History, evolution, community and matter.

History: Hinduism is often said to possess no sense of history.
What can be safely asserted with less fear of overgeneralization
is that Hinduism sets no ultimate value on history the way
Western religions tend to do. Aurobindo is perhaps unique in
that he offers a systematic analysis of Indian history[16] with a
view to determining its role in the world. He identifies three
characteristics of Indian culture: (1) spirituality, (2) creativity
and (3) intellectuality. "Consequently, when the decline came,
all these three powers gradually deteriorated. First, the creative power declined, then the critical mind ceased to function

[14]Ibid., p. 363. "Before his death (5 December, 1950), Sri Aurobindo had the idea of establishing an international city based on the
concept of the spiritual unity of mankind" (V. S. Naravane, op. cit.,
p. 198).

[15]One could, for instance, relate his philosophy to that of Sankara
(see D. S. Sarma, op. cit., p. 333; T. M. P. Mahadevan, *Outlines of
Hinduism* [Bombay: Chetana Ltd, 1960] p. 233; etc.). One could also
focus on his contribution to the study of the Bhagavadgita (D. S.
Sarma, op. cit., pp. 321-324); look upon him as reviving the Tantrika
tradition or making his contribution to Yoga in the form of Yoga
Integral (see Thomas J. Hopkins, op. cit., pp. 138-139; more specially
Kees W. Bolle, *The Persistence of Religion: an essay on Tantrish and Sri
Aurobindo's philosophy* (Leiden : E. J. Brill, 1925).

[16]See D. S. Sarma, op. cit., pp. 313-318.

and, finally our spirituality became diseased."[17] Of these three characteristics spirituality[18] is primary. "The question now is. . . whether the spiritual motive which has shaped her civilization or the intellectual motive which shaped the civilization of ancient Europe or the economic motive which is shaping the civilization of modern Europe is to be the leading motive of human culture."[19] Aurobindo recommends that, the spiritual motive should shape modern culture and spirituality being India's primary characteristic, her role in this context is obviously one of great importance. In order to fulfil this role India must practise "aggressive defence." "And an aggressive defence implies, in the circumstances, three things. Firstly, it implies a new creation, i.e. a bringing of what we have to greater force of form. Secondly, it implies an effective assimilation of whatever is useful for our new life and is harmonious with the spirit of our culture. And, thirdly, it implies our meeting modern problems with solutions different from those offered by the West—solutions which will effectively justify our own ideals. But to do this we must be well grounded in our own culture and be thoroughly conversant with all its implications. Śrī Aurobindo points out that it is only a man who lives completely from his own inner self that can go out and embrace the universal, it is only a true Svarāt that can become a true Samrat."[20]

Evolution: The doctrine of evolution as developed by modern science is a new category whose emergence created theological difficulties for Christianity. Some Western thinkers have tried to integrate it with Christian thought,[21] Aurobindo seems to be attempting to do the same for Hindu thought.[22] The significance of such an enterprise needs to be more fully grasped.

[17]Ibid., p. 315.

[18]Ibid., p. 314.

[19]Ibid,, p.316.

[20]Ibid., p. 317:318. See Aurobindo Ghose, *The Renaissance of India* (Chandranagore: Prabartak Publishing House, 1920).

[21]See R. C. Zaehner, *Evolution in Religion: a study in Sri Aurobindo and Pierre Teilhard de Chardin* (Oxford: Clarendon Press, 1971).

[22]It has been suggested that the doctrine of the incarnations of Visnu seems to anticipate the doctrine of evolution, if the major *avataras* are related to evolutionary 'leaps'.

Normally, when a thinker or a theologian sets out to reflect on the nature of the universe and our place in it in pre-modern times, he had only one major datum to account for—the existence of the world. Now, however, when he embarks on a similar enterprise and takes the scientific account of the emergence of earth and life on it seriously, he has two data to account for (1) the existence of the world and (2) the fact of evolution. Similarly, the other great datum the theologian or thinker had to account for was man—or his presence as a part of the world. Here again, whereas earlier on he had to account for only the existence of life, he has now to account for two data: (1) the existence of life and (2) the fact of its evolution. Thus the question of evolution comes to assume primary significance from a theological and philosophical point of view in modern times, unless one chooses to simply brush it aside.

In Aurobindo's system Pure Existent (Sat), Consciousness-Force (Cit), Delight of Existence (Ānanda), Supermind, Mind, Life and Matter "Constitute the sevenfold chord of Being."[23] Now according to D. S. Sarma we have "in a nutshell, the whole of Śrī Aurobindo philosophy"[24] in this passage:

The Divine descends from pure Existence through the play of Consciousness-Force and Bliss and the creative medium of supermind into cosmic being; we ascend from matter through a developing life, soul and mind and the illuminating medium of supermind towards the divine being. The knot of the two, the higher and the lower hemisphere, is where mind and supermind meet with a veil between them. The rending of the veil is the condition of the divine life in humanity; for by that rending, by the illuminating descent of the higher into the nature of the lower being and the forceful ascent of the lower being into the nature of the higher, mind can recover its divine light in the all-comprehending supermind, the soul realise its divine self in the all-possessing, all-blissful Ānanda, life repossess its divine power in the play of omniscient Consciousness-Force and matter open to its divine liberty as a form of the Divine Existence.[25]

[23]T. M. P. Mahadevan, op. cit., p. 234.
[24]D. S. Sarma, op. cit., p. 327.
[25]Ibid.

It is clear that the movement described in this passage can
be metaphysically viewed as one of evolution and involution
but can be 'scientifically' viewed as one representing the next
step in evolution, in the sense that man's evolution, which has
hitherto been biological, is now seen as proceeding along spiritual lines.[26]

Community and Matter: It has often been asserted about Hinduism that in it the individual has priority over the communal
and the spiritual over the material. Although these statements
have become clichés they seem to contain an element of truth
according to Aurobindo, especially in view of India's actual
condition as he found it.[27] It need hardly be added that these
dimensions—the communal and the material—are strongly
represented in Western life and thought and widely recognized
as so represented. Aurobindo's interpretation of Hindu
thought strengthens these elements within it, as will be clear
from the following statement of his thought:

> There is a double movement at work in Reality, says Śrī
> Aurobindo, a descent and an ascent. 'The Divine descends
> from pure existence through the play of Consciousness-
> Force and Bliss and the creative medium of Supermind
> into cosmic being; we ascend from Matter through a develop-
> ing life, soul and mind, and the illuminating medium of
> Supermind towards the Divine Being.' These two movements
> are really complementary to each other; there is no contra-
> diction between them. The ascension enables the divine
> descent; the descent fulfils that for which the ascension as-
> pires and which it makes inevitable. In the past, saints and
> sages have risen from the lower levels to the higher. But they
> did not attempt, says Śrī Aurobindo, to bring the Supermind
> down into the consciousness of the earth and make it fixed
> there. To so bring it down is the aim of Śrī Aurobindo's *Yoga*.[28]

It should be noted, firstly, that the Supermind is visualized
as coming down to the earth, as descending to the lower chord

[26]Sri Aurobindo, *The Life Divine* Book Two Part Two (Pondicherry:
Sri Aurobindo Ashram Trust, 1977) p. 1069—1070.

[27]Ibid., p.317.

[28]T. M. P. Mahadevan, op. cit., p. 238—239.

of being. Matter is receiving the 'spirit' so to say. Hence the
negative association of "matter" is overcome.[29] Secondly, this
descent is visualized as taking place in the experience of the
community as a whole. It is not a case of a few individuals
going up into the spiritual realm but the limits of the realm
itself extending to cover the human race. Thus the communal
dimension of the event is celebrated. "Aurobindo's concern
with the social results of mystical intuition are in rather striking
contrast to that of many other mystics. As man developed, he
argued, he would become 'acutely aware of the discord and
ignorance that governs his relation with the world, acutely
intolerant of it, more and more set on finding a principle of
harmony, peace, joy, and unity."[30]

[29]See Aurobindo Ghose, *The Future Evolution of Man: the divine life
upon earth* (New York: Humanities Press, 1963).

[30]Ainslie T. Embree, ed., op. cit., p. 334, Attention may also be
drawn to the following eschatological vision of Aurobindo:

The meeting of man and God must always mean a penetration and
entry of the Divine into the human and a self-immergence of man
in the Divinity.

But that immergence is not in the nature of an annihilation.
Extinction is not the fulfilment of all this search and passion, suffering and rapture. The game would never have been begun if that
were to be its ending.

Delight is the secret. Learn of pure delight and thou shalt learn of
God.

What then was the commencement of the whole matter? Existence
that multiplied itself for sheer delight of being and plunged into
numberless trillions of forms so that it might find itself innumerably.
And what is the middle? Division that strives towards a multiple
unity, ignorance that labours towards a flood of varied light, pain
that travails towards the touch of an unimaginable ecstasy. For all
these things are dark figures and perverse vibrations.

And what is the end of the whole matter? As if honey could taste
itself and all its drops together and all its drops could taste each
other and each the whole honeycomb as itself, so should the end
be with God and the soul of man and the universe.

Love is the key-note, Joy is the music, Power is the strain, Knowledge is the performer, the infinite All is the composer and audience.
We know only the preliminary discords which are as fierce as the
harmony shall be great; but we shall arrive surely at the fugue of
the divine Beatitudes.

(Sri Aurobindo Ghose, *Collected Works,* Vol. 16 (Pondicherry:
Aurobindo Ashram), p. 384)

D. SUMMARY

In the case of both Tagore and Aurobindo their internationalism finally got the better of their nationalism whether political or religious. Both became non-political after flirting with political nationalism for a while and so far as religious nationalism is concerned in the case of one it became highly moral and in the case of the other metaphysical. Next we turn to the study of Gandhi in whom the two nationalisms were held together bounded by an overall internationalism—in synthesis, compromise, tension or confusion, as you please.

Mahatma Gandhi

It is difficult to write about Mohandas Karamchand Gandhi
(1869-1948), popularly known as Mahatma Gandhi, because he
wrote so much himself[1] and because so much has been written
about him.[2] But one cannot afford to overlook the life and
thought of someone who is known "to the world as the greatest
Indian of modern times."[3]

In analysing the thought of Mahatma Gandhi, in the context of religious ferment in modern India, it is particularly important to pay attention to his life. There are several reasons
for adopting such an attitude. Firstly, "He himself declared,
when asked for his message to mankind, 'My life is my message'."[4] Secondly, "Harmony between thought and deed meant
far more to Gāndhi than consistency between one thought and
another."[5] Thirdly, truth for Gandhi was not a system of
abstract thought, rather he felt called upon "to be faithful to
truth he saw it *at the moment*"[6]—his life being a series of such
moments. Fourthly, not only was truth for Gandhi something
not abstract, it wasn't something fixed, not in the sense that
there could be no abiding values but rather in the sens e that in

---

[1]*The New Encyclopaedia Britannica*, Macropedia Vol. 7 (Chicago:
Helen Hemingway Benton, 1974) p. 878.

[2]Jagdish Sharan Sharma, *Mahatma Gandhi: a descriptive biblio-
graphy* (Delhi: So Chand, 1968).

[3] Wm. Theodore de Bary, op. cit., p. 247.

[4]Ibid.

[5]Ibid.

[6]Ibid., p. 251, emphasis added.

the application of these values to life 'new occasions teach new duties'.

This virtually total interpenetration of theory and practice at least partly explains the problem one encounters in dealing with the thought of Gandhi.[7] His contradictions drew C.F. Andrews into speaking of his "infantile confusion of thought."[8] T.W. Organ cites a typical example of these contradictions. On August 25, 1920 he said that violence is preferable to cowardice but on February 16, 1922 he said: "It is better to be charged with cowardice and weakness than to be guilty of violating our oath [of truth and non-violence]."[9] The fact is that "he 'experimented' with truth no less than with diet, dress and medicine."[10] Finally, there was "nothing adventurous about Gandhi the thinker,"[11] it was his life which was full of adventures in the best sense of the word.

A. LIFE

The life of Mahatma Gandhi falls into four chronologically clear segments :

1869-1888   early life in India
1888-1891   student's life in England
1891-1915   life in South Africa first as a lawyer and then as a leader
1915-1948   national figure in India and subsequently leader in the struggle for Independence

In the first phase of his life Gandhi absorbed the vaiṣṇava and Jain influences current in Gujarat. It is an interesting fact that he had to take the vows of abstaining from meat, women and wine before his mother would let him travel to England[12] and it is

[7]V. S. Naravane, op, cit., p. 161.

[8]Quoted in Troy Wilson Organ, op. cit., p. 364.

[9]Ibid., p. 364. It could be argued, though, that the contradiction here is apparent than real.

[10]V. S. Naravane, op. cit., p. 160.

[11]Ibid.

[12]Mahadev Desai, tr., *M. K. Gandhi An Autobiography* (London: Jonathan Cape, 1972) p. 33.

of further interest that these vows were administered to him by
a Jain monk.[13] By the time he left for England at the age of
eighteen "his mind had been deeply and permanently molded
by traditional Indian influences."[14]

In England Gandhi encountered European influences, particularly Christianity. He studied the Bible and the Bhagavadgītā
and had cordial relations with several Englishmen. After com-
pleting his studies he returned to India. In 1891, however,
Gandhi was invited to South Africa as a lawyer by a Muslim
client and it is here that certain decisive developments took
place.

Africa was to present to Gandhi challenges and opportuni-
ties that he could hardly have conceived. In a Durban
court, he was asked by the European magistrate to take off
his turban; he refused, and left the courtroom. A few days
later, while travelling to Pretoria, he was unceremoniously
thrown out of a first-class railway compartment and left
shivering and brooding at Pietermaritzburg Station; in the
further course of the journey he was beaten up by the white
driver of a stage-coach because he would not travel on the
footboard to make room for a European passenger; and
finally he was barred from hotels reserved "for Europeans
only." These humiliations were the daily lot of Indian
traders and labourers in Natal who had learned to pocket
them with the same resignation with which they pocketed
their meagre earnings. What was new was not Gandhi's
experience, but his reaction. He had so far not been
conspicuous for self-assertion or aggressiveness. But something happened to him as he smarted under the insults heap-
ed upon him. In retrospect the journey from Durban to
Pretoria struck him as one of the most creative experiences
of his life; it was his moment of truth. Henceforth he would
not accept injustice as part of the natural or unnatural order
in South Africa; he would defend his dignity as an Indian
and as a man.[15]

[13]Ibid.
[14]Wm. Theodore de Bary, op. cit., p. 248.
[15]*The New Encyclopaedia Britannica*, op. cit., p. 875.

In 1915 Gandhi returned to India and by 1920 had come to the fore of the nationalist movement against British Rule. He directed three major campaigns against it: 1920-22; 1930-34 and 1940-42. The technique he employed against the British Raj was one of Satyāgraha[16] a word which literally means "firmness in truth" and actually meant passive resistance. We have the following eye-witness account of his famous Salt Satyāgraha from Mr. Webb Miller, an American correspondent of the events of May 21, 1930, which gives us a glimpse of Gandhi's technique at work :

Mme. Naidu called for prayer before the march started and the entire assemblage knelt. She exhorted them: 'Gandhi's body is in jail but his soul is with you. India's prestige is in

[16]T. M. P. Mahadevan (op. cit., p. 230-231) writes: "Two aspects may be distinguished in Gāndhi's programme of *satyāgraha* These are: non-violent non-cooperation and civil disobedience. The former of these is the method of refusal to associate oneself with wrong. In the realm of politics it means the withdrawal of cooperation from a wicked ruler so that he may be weaned from his wickedness. Any tyrannical political system functions because of the tacit submission to it by the people over whom it has power. If the people resolve not to co-operate with it, then it cannot succeed. Under the category of non-cooperation falls Gāndhi's advice to the Indian nation, in 1920, of withdrawal of children from schools and colleges owned or aided by the Government, boycott of the British courts by lawyers and litigants, etc. But non-cooperation is only a step to the other aspect of *satyāgraha*, viz., civil disobedience, an expression which was first used by Thoreau. Civil disobedience is rebellion against the laws of the unjust state. The breaking of the salt law in 1930—a law which was most obnoxious, according to Gāndhi, because it taxed one of the primary necessities of life—and the various no-tax campaigns are instances of civil disobedience. But whatever be the method a *satyāgrahi* adopts against the government, he must remain peaceful and non-violent and suffer the consequences of his disobedience cheerfully and with no regrets. This requires, of course, discipline and self-control. If the method of violence takes plenty of training, the method of non-violence must take even more training. To train his soldiers in non-violence Gāndhi gave them a constructive programme. In this programme were included such activities as removal of illiteracy, revival of village industries, adoption of the simple life, etc. And, as the basic foundation of the training, he exhorted his followers to have a living faith in God."

your hands, you must not use any violence under any circumstances. You will be beaten but you must not resist; you
must not even raise a hand to ward off blows.' Wild, shrill
cheers terminated her speech.

Slowly and in silence the throng commenced the half-mile
march to salt-deposits. A few carried ropes for lassoing the
barbed-wire stockade around the salt pans. About a score
who were assigned to act as stretcher-bearers wore crude,
hand-painted red crosses pinned to their breasts, their stretchers consisted of blankets. Manilal Gandhi, second son of
Gandhi, walked among the foremost of the marchers. As
the throng drew near the salt pans they commenced chant-
ing the revolutionary slogans, *Inquilab Zindabad*, intoning
the two words over and over.

The salt-deposits were surrounded by ditches filled with
water and guarded by four hundred native Surat Police in
Khaki shorts and brown turbans. Half a dozen British officials
commanded them. The Police carried *lathis*—five foot clubs
tipped with steel. Inside the stockade twenty-five native
rifle-men were drawn up.

In complete silence the Gandhi men drew up and halted a
hundred yards from the stockade. A picked column advanced from the crowd, waded the ditches, and approached
the barbed-wire stockade, which the Surat Police surrounded, holding clubs at the ready. Police officials ordered the
marchers to disperse under a recently imposed regulation
which prohibited gathering of more than five persons in any
one place. The column silently ignored the warning and
slowly walked forward. I stayed with the main body about
a hundred yards from the stockade.

Suddenly, at a word of command, scores of native police
rushed upon the advancing marchers and rained blows on
their heads with their steel-shod *lathis*. Not one of the
marchers even raised an arm to fend off the blows. They
went down like ten-pins. From where I stood I heard the
sickening whacks of the clubs on unprotected skulls. The
waiting crowd of watchers groaned and sucked in their
breaths in sympathetic pain at every blow.

Those struck down fell sprawling, unconscious or writhing
in pain with fractured skulls or broken shoulders. In two

or three minutes the ground was quilted with bodies. Great patches of blood widened on their white clothes. The survivors, without breaking ranks, silently and doggedly marched on until struck down. When everyone of the first column had been knocked down, stretcher-bearers rushed up unmolested by the Police and carried off the injured to a thatched hut which had been arranged as a temporary hospital.

Then another column formed while the leaders pleaded with them to retain their self-control. They marched slowly towards the police. Although everyone knew that within a few minutes he would be beaten down, perhaps killed, I could detect no signs of wavering or fear. They marched steadily with heads up, without the encouragement of music or cheering or any possibility that they might escape serious injury or death. The police rushed out and methodically and mechanically beat down the second column. There was no fight, no struggle; the marchers simply walked forward until struck down. There were no outcries, only groans after they fell. There were not enough stretcher-bearers to carry off the wounded; I saw eighteen injured being carried off simultaneously, while forty-two still lay bleeding on the ground awaiting stretcher-bearers. The blankets used as stretchers were sodden with blood.[17]

Gandhi's efforts were crowned with success in 1947 when India achieved Independence but this achievement was flawed by Hindu-Muslim riots and the partition of the country into India and Pakistan. Gandhi worked for rapprochement between the two countries and regimes but was assassinated by a Hindu for being pro-Muslim, on January 30, 1948:

It was nearly ten past five. They came out on open grass and climbed the steps to the garden prayer ground. Several hundred people were waiting. Most of them stood up. Those directly in front of Gandhi parted each way to make a lane, some bowing to his feet as he went by. He took his arms off the girls' shoulders and raised them in greeting.

[17]In R. C. Majumdar, ed., *Struggle for Freedom* (Bombay: Bharatiya Vidya Bhavan, 1969) p. 471-472.

Suddenly a man in a khaki jacket pushed through from the right. It was the conspirator Godse. Manu thought he was a pilgrim prostrating himself in the Mahatma's path, and as they were late, she put out a hand to check him. He thrust her away so hard that she stumbled. Two feet from Gandhi he actually did make a brief bow. Then he raised a pistol and fired three shots. The first bullet entered Gandhi's abdomen and came out through his back. It caught him in mid-stride. His foot touched the ground but he stayed upright. The second passed between his ribs and also came out at the back. A bloodstain appeared on his white shawl. His hands sank. The third bullet struck his chest above the right nipple and lodged in the lung. His face turned grey. His left forearm returned for a moment to Abha's shoulder. In these last instants, bystanders heard him gasping the divine name Rama. Then he crumpled and fell backwards, his glasses dropping off, his sandals coming away from his feet.

The gardener recovered soonest. He seized Godse and held him till others dragged him off into custody. Gandhi was carried indoors. Patel, who had not yet left the grounds, rushed back and felt his pulse. Pyarelal telephoned for a doctor. He came in ten minutes but could do nothing. All was over, quickly and mercifully.[18]

B. GANDHI AND NATIONALISM

In this part of the book we have tried to look at religious ferment in modern India in terms of the rise of nationalism in India and in doing so have tried to relate it to internationalism as well. We have also tried to examine the interaction of religious and political nationalism. The position of Gandhi on these points may now be analyzed.

Was Gandhi a nationalist or an internationalist? The entry in the New Encyclopaedia Britannica under his name describes him as the "pre-eminent leader of Indian nationalism"[19] at the beginning but says towards the end: "It is probably too

---

[18]Geoffrey Ashe, *Gandhi: A Study in Revolution* (London: Heinemann, 1968) p. 382-383.
[19]p. 874.

early to judge Gandhi's place in history. He was the catalyst
if not the initiator of three of the major revolutions of the
twentieth century: the revolution against colonialism, racism
and violence."[20] Thus although the locus of Gandhi's work was
India, its focus was universal. Unlike Tagore and Aurobindo,
who may have moved from nationalism towards internationalism, Gandhi functioned at the national level while retaining
in and imparting to his work an international dimension. One
of his oft-quoted statements on the question of rival cultural
influences is also one of his best: "I do not want my house to
be walled in on all sides and my windows to be stuffed. I want
the cultures of all lands to be blown about my house as freely
as possible. But I refuse to be blown off my feet"[21] by any.
This should not lead the reader to conclude, however, that
Gandhi had not absorbed Western influences.[22]

The interaction between religious and political nationalism
in Gandhi presents a slight problem. There is a difference of
opinion among scholars as to which of the two elements was
primary. Thus it has been said that the "key to understanding
Gandhi is the fact that he was first, last, and always a politician."[23] The fact that Gandhi once said of himself: "Men
say I am a saint losing myself in politics. The fact is I am a
politician trying my hardest to be a saint,"[24] seems to lend
support to this view. On the other hand, it has been suggested
that Gandhi's deepest strivings were spiritual, but unlike many
of his countrymen with such aspirations, he did not retire to
a cave in the Himalayas to meditate on the Absolute; he carried
his cave, as he once said, with him. For him truth was not
something to be discovered in the privacy of one's personal
life; it had to be upheld in the challenging contexts of social
and political life."[25] A third approach is sometimes suggested,
bicameral in nature. On this view Gandhi functioned at both
the political and the religious level and "Because his mind

[20]p. 878.
[21]Quoted by Troy Wilson Organ, op. cit., p. 370.
[22]See L. S. S. O'Malley, op. cit., p. 97; V. S. Naravane, op. cit.,
p. 164; etc.
[23]Troy Wilson Organ, op. cit., p. 366.
[24]Quoted in Wm. Theodore de Bary, op. cit., p. 250.
[25]*The New Encyclopaedia Britannica*, p. 878.

operated in two different dimensions—the religious, with its
insistence on absolute perfection and purity, and the political,
with its emphasis on practicality and expediency—he often
seemed to contradict himself."[26] Finally, a fourth approach
may be suggested—that from a Gandhian point of view the
distinction between religion and politics may be artificial.[27]
Perhaps a variety of explanations is required to deal with the
complexity of the relationship between religious and political
nationalism in the person of Gandhi. No final answers seem
possible at this stage but the issue is crucial. There is a school
of histo.ians which maintains that Gandhi Hinduized the
national movement which should have been allowed to proceed
along purely political, i.e. constitutional lines and that this
would have prevented the partition of the country. Another
school maintains that this represents a naive view of the British
Raj in India, that without a mass-movement the British strang-
lehold on India could not have been broken and that the blame
for the Partition must be borne by the British and certain sections
of the Muslim and Hindu communities, and not by Gandhi.

C. GANDHI AND HINDUISM

Gandhi was both a product and an agent of religious ferment
in India, specially in relation to Hinduism. He was a product
in the sense that while remaining within the tradition he did not
hesitate to question such aspects of it he did not approve of. In
remaining within the tradition yet freely criticizing it he reflected
the spirit of such predecessors as Raja Rammohun Roy, Swami
Dayananda, Swami Vivekananda, etc. His attitude towards
Christianity represented the same heritage—like Dayananda
he was critical of Christian proselytization[28] (though he did
not approve of reconversion to Hinduism) and like Roy and
Vivekananda he rejected Christianity but accepted Christ.[29]
Moreover, like his predecessors he was selective in his approach
towards Hindu scriptures. It may be too cynical to suggest that

[26]Wm. Theodore de Bary, op. cit., p. 250.
[27]Mahadev Desai, tr., op. cit. p. XII, 419-420.
[28]D. S. Sarma op. cit., p. 573.
[29]L. S. S. O'Malley, ed., op. cit., p. 334-336.

he had a prefabricated ideology for which he sought scriptural sanction. Such a view would overlook the interaction that seemed to take place between him and the scriptures such as the Bhagavadgītā. But there is little doubt that in his scheme scriptures took second place to reason and conscience. When they went against his cherished views of human dignity and spirituality he was prepared to reject them. Thus he recommended the rejection of certain passages as interpolations[30] and even declared: "If I discovered that the Vedas clearly showed that they claimed divine authority for untouchability, then nothing on this earth would hold me to Hinduism. I would throw it overboard like a rotten apple."[31] On the other hand such scriptural passages as conformed to a certain spirituality evoked his whole-hearted admiration. He wrote in 1937: "I have now come to the final conclusion that if all the Upanisads and all the other scriptures happened all of a sudden to be reduced to ashes and if only the first verse in the Iśopanisad were left intact in the memory of the Hindus, Hinduism will live forever."[32] He also expressed the wish that he had "no other wish in this world but to find light and joy and peace through Hinduism."[33]

What was this Hinduism which so appealed to him? He wrote in 1946 that "There are two aspects of Hinduism. There is, on the one hand, the historical Hinduism with its untouchability, superstitious worship of stocks and stones, animal sacrifices and so on. On the other, we have the Hinduism of the *Gita*, the *Upanishads*, and Patanjali *Yoga Sutras* which is the acme of *Ahimsa* and oneness of all creation, pure worship of one immanent, formless, imperishable God."[34] Gandhi here implicitly distinguishes between a lower and a higher Hinduism. He tried to cultivate the latter and reform the former. Let us first examine his attitude of lower Hinduism.

The aspect of lower Hinduism he disliked most was Untouchability—and next to it the iniquitous aspects of the caste system. Untouchability he attacked head on, and his "campaign

[30]Troy Wilson Organ, op. cit., p. 364-365.
[31]Quoted Ibid., p. 365.
[32]As quoted in T. M. P. Mahadevan, op. cit., p. 26.
[33]Ibid., p. vi.
[34]Quoted in Troy Wilson Organ, op. cit., p. 368.

against untouchability" in the opinion of one modern Hindu
scholar "is the greatest service he has rendered to Hinduism."[35]
His attack on caste discrimination was also quite sustained.
A. L. Basham has remarked:

The earlier reformers had but laid the foundations—Gāndhī
was the real architect of the new Hinduism. When he died
Hinduism had largely reorientated itself. Caste and the ideas
of ritual pollution which go with it, are present still, but
those educated Hindus who still retain the more obvious
caste prejudices do so rather shamefacedly, and against their
better judgment. For Gāndhī not only preached human equality, but practised it when he persuaded his followers to
perform for themselves the menial tasks normally reserved
for out-castes, even to emptying latrines, he sounded the
death-knell of untouchability and the whole caste system.[36]

As for higher Hinduism, he accepted its teachings but in an
experientially deepened and eclectically widened version. Thus
he wrote: "I have endeavoured in the light of prayerful study
of the other faiths of the world, and what is more, in the light
of my own experiences in trying to live the teachings of Hinduism, . . . to give an extended but by no means strained meaning
to Hinduism, not as buried in its ample scriptures, but as a
living faith speaking like a mother to her aching children".[37]
In this way he also tried to integrate 'scriptural' Hinduism with
'historical' Hinduism by trying "to find sanction for a revolutionary social ethic within the Hindu tradition."[38]

The two virtues which Gandhi selected out of the higher
Hinduism for special emphasis and cultivation were TRUTH
(satya) and NON-VIOLENCE (Ahimsā), which are "so inter-
twined that it is difficult to separate them. They are like two
sides of a coin or rather a smooth unstamped metallic disc.
Who can say which is the obverse and which is the reverse?
Nevertheless Ahimsā is the means, Truth is the end."[39] "Truth

[35]D. S. Sarma, op. cit., p. 575.
[36]R. C. Zaehner, ed., op. cit., p. 259.
[37]Quoted in Ainslie T. Embree, ed., op. cit., p. 339.
[38]Ibid., p. 328.
[39]Quoted by D. S. Sarma, op. cit., p. 568.

and non-violence, then, constitute the twin principle of Gandhian philosophy. Hinduism was once defined by Gandhi as 'search after truth through non-violent means'. It may be said that this is no definition of Hinduism, since the statement would be true of every religion. But that is exactly what Hinduism claims, viz., that the truth of every religion is the same."[40]

Truth and non-violence are well-known rules of moral conduct but by giving them the centrality in his life and work which he accorded to them, Gandhi achieved a singular result. He identified religion with morality and thus helped raise the moral tone of Hinduism and Indian national life. "Building on the work of previous reformers, but chiefly relying on his own genius for creative improvisation, he gave the Indian independence movement a quality unique in human history. Nonviolence, *ahimsa*, was more than a technique to be used by the weak *against* the strong: it was primarily a way of life, of which political freedom was but one manifestation."[41]

The practical expression of *ahimsa* was *satyagraha*. Herein the chief contribution of Gandhi lies in showing "to the world that truth and non-violence could be employed as weapons to achieve political and social ends, and that in such employment lay the salvation of humanity. Religious reformers before Gandhi had taught that truth and non-violence were primarily religious virtues fit to be practised by the competent few. Private individuals and small communities have, in the past, adopted these precepts for governing their own lives. But the revolution that Gandhi effected was with regard to men's conception of politics."[42]

D. CONCLUSION

It is not easy to satisfactorily conclude a discussion on Gandhi. For our purposes, however, suffice it to say that Gandhi succeeded to the extent that he could successfully identify political nationalism with religious nationalism where religion means morality and failed to the extent that this identification of political and religious nationalism could not always be confined to the level of morality.

[40]T. M. P. Mahadevan, op. cit., p. 227.
[41]Ainslie T. Embree, ed., op. cit., p. 328.
[42]T. M. P. Mahadevan, op. cit., p. 228.

Muhammad Iqbal

Undivided India had the world's largest population of both
Hindus and Muslims, although Muslims constituted about a
quarter of the total population of India. The previous chapters
covered the rise of political nationalism and its interaction with
religious nationalism, by and large, in the Hindu context. It is now
time to consider the rise of political nationalism and its interaction with religious nationalism in the case of Islam in India
in the twentieth century. The working of these forces is perhaps
best exemplified in the life and thought of Muhammad Iqbal
(1873—1938), in whom "we have a poet-philosopher whose
status in modern Indian literature ranks next only to Tagore's,
and who was at the same time fully initiated in the discipline of
technical philosophy. With the exception of Radhakrishnan, no
other Indian thinker of the modern age had the qualifications of
a 'professional philosopher' to the extent that Iqbal had."[1] Iqbal
thus was essentially an academic, a poet and a philosopher,
though he did take to law and politics at times.[2] It is, however,
not so much his forays into politics as the political implications
of his thought which have made him something of a controversial figure. Two main points of view are encountered in
this connection. According to one: "Sir Syed had brought
rationalism and the desire for knowledge and progress to the
Indian Muslims; Iqbal brought them inspiration and a philosophy.
Next to the Qur'ān, there is no single influence upon the
consciousness of the Pakistani intelligentsia so powerful as

[1]V.S. Naravane, op. cit., p. 271.
[2]Wm. Theodore de Bary, ed., op. cit., p. 197, 199.

Iqbal's poetry. In his own time it kindled the enthusiasm of
Muslim intellectuals for the values of Islam, and rallied the
whole Muslim community once again to the banner of their
faith. For this reason Iqbal is looked upon today as the
spiritual founder of Pakistan."[3] From another standpoint,
"Iqbal's incursion into political life has been a subject of
controversy among historians of modern India. He was elected
to the Punjab Legislative Assembly and was invited to the
Round Table Conference in England. But on the whole he was
not attracted towards politics or politicians. An interesting
anecdote bears this out. A few months before his death Iqbal
expressed a desire to meet Jawaharlal Nehru, who responded
with pleasure. During their conversation Iqbal said to Nehru:
'What is there in common between you and Jinnah. You are a
patriot, while he is a politician.' Iqbal's deep feeling for the
unity of the Islamic world, and his concern for the future of
Indian Muslims, sometimes led him to take positions which
strengthened the separate elements in Indian politics. But to
describe him as the 'spiritual founder of Pakistan' is manifestly
an exaggeration."[4]

This controversy itself testifies to the complexity, if not the
ambiguity, of the interaction of political and religious nationalisms in the case of the Muslim community in India. The
contours of the controversy are seen more clearly in the following context. Rabindranath Tagore wrote in 1923: "When,
with the coming of the new age, the Hindu was roused to a
sense of dignity in his Hinduism, if the Muslim had simply
acquiesced therein it would have doubtless suited us admirably.
But the same causes likewise roused the Muslim to a sense of
dignity in Islam."[5] Thus one of the main issues in the first half
of the twentieth century, with the rise of nationalism (apart from
that of dislodging the British from India) was to evolve a
formula which could contain the political and religious nationalisms of both the Hindu and Muslim communities. The hope
was that the two communities could be politically united by an
Indian nationalism and their religious nationalism could be

[3]Ibid., p. 197, emphasis added.
[4]V.S. Naravane, op. cit., p. 277-278.
[5]Ibid., p. 271.

reconciled through the concept of a secular state. The Muslim
fears of being swamped by a Hindu majority in a parliamentary
form of government could not be allayed successfully[6] and thus
the country had to be divided. But as the case of Iqbal and the
contrasts between his Tarana-e-Hind (Anthem of India) and
his clarion calls on behalf of pan-Islamicism indicate—the issue
was in doubt for quite some time and the fact that India
continues to be a secular state with almost as many Muslims as
there are in Pakistan (after the separation of Bangla Desh)
seems to indicate that it has not yet been fully resolved.

It is, however, to Iqbal's thought in itself that we must now
turn. It is to be found in his poetic works in Urdu and Persian
such as Bang-e-Dara (Caravan Bells), Asrar-e-Khudi (Secrets
of the Self), etc.; and in his works in English, such as The
Development of Metaphysics in Persia and The Reconstruction
of Religious Thought in Islam.[7]

A. IQBAL AND THE WEST

As with so many other Indian thinkers, Western thought
exerted considerable influence on Iqbal. He was "particularly
influenced by Nietzsche and Bergson."[8] Nietzsche's concept
of the superman seems to have been a source of his poetic
inspiration. "His theme was the all-embracing sufficiency of
Islam as expressing a dynamic spirit of struggle for spiritual
freedom. Islam was not merely a valid religion to be compared
favourably with others; it was the root and branch of all
religious experience. It was not a fixed and precious deposit
to be treasured with the zeal of the antiquarian, but a living
principle of action which could give purpose and remake
worlds. Europe was enmeshed in its greed for wealth and lust
for power. It was for Islam to create true values and to assert

[6]See Percival Spear, op. cit., p. 361.

[7]The statement that he "only produced one work in English"
seems to be incorrect (Percival Spear, op. cit., p. 366). V.S. Naravane
(op. cit., p. 278) seems to discount the significance of his prose works
unduly in the context of his thought, see Kenneth Cragg, The House
of Islam (Belmont, California: Dickenson Publishing Co., 1975) p. 119.

[8]Wm. Theodore de Bary, ed., op. cit., p. 197; also see H.A.R.
Gibb, Mohammedanism (Oxford University Press, 1969) p. 126.

man's mastery of nature by constant struggle. It was Nietszche in an Islamic setting."[9]

Having said this, however, one must now set about qualifying the statements made above. Firstly, although Iqbal was influenced by the West, he was not an uncritical admirer of the West. His opinion of the West is given in the following two couplets:

[9]Percival Spear, op. cit., P. 361 Seyyed Hossein Nasr thinks that Iqbal's identification of the Sufi idea of the Perfect Man (al-insan al-kamil) and the Nietzschean idea of the superman was a "great mistake" (*Islam and the Plight of Modern Man* [London: Longman, 1975] p. 146). From our point of view, however, the important point to recognize is that "When so original and revolutionary a thinker as the late Sir Muhammad Iqbal desired to popularise his ideas of Man and Superman, not only did he turn back to Rūmī and the mediaeval mystics to discover antecedents within Islam for the system for which he sought acceptance, but he cast his thoughts in the mould of Sufi allegory that has been sanctified by centuries of Persian poetry.

> In my heart's empire, see
> How he rides spitefully,
> Rides with imperious will
> To ravage, and to kill;
>
> No heart is there, but bright
> Gleameth in that moon's light,
> A thousand mirrors, see;
> Reflect his coquetry.
>
> To each hand he hath won
> Ten realms of Solomon,
> Yet gambles with it all
> To gain a mean, poor thrall.
>
> The hearts of such as know
> Swift he assaults; but lo!
> Before the unwise, unskilled
> He casteth down his shield.
>> (A.J. Arberry, *Sufism* [London: George Allen & Unwin Ltd, 1975] p. 133).

Also see Hafeez Malik, ed., *Iqbal Poet-Philosopher of Pakistan* (New York: Columbia University Press, 1971).

> 'The glitter of modern civilization dazzles
>   the sight,
> But it is only a clever piecing together of
>   false gems'
> 'The wisdom or science in which the wise ones of
>   the West took such pride
> Is but a warring sword in the bloody hands of
>   greed and ambition.' [10]

Secondly, while Iqbal glorifies self-assertion, he is opposed to undisciplined individualism, which he regards as an attribute of modern Western capitalism. Thirdly, he is opposed to nationalism, like Tagore:

> Now brotherhood has been so cut to shreds
> That in the stead of community
> The country has been given pride of place
> In men's allegiance and constructive work;
> The country is the darling of their hearts,
> And wide humanity is whittled down
> Into dismembered tribes. . . .
> Vanished is humankind; there but abide
> The disunited nations. Politics
> Dethroned religion. . . . [11]

Unlike Tagore, however, he finds the answer to the bane of nationalism not in Humanism or the Religion of Man but in pan-Islamicism or the religion of Islam.

> Our Essence is not bound to any place;
> The vigor of our wine is not contained
> In any bowl; Chinese and Indian
> Alike the shard that constitutes our jar,
> Turkish and Syrian alike the clay
> Forming our body; neither is our heart
> Of India, or Syria, or Rum,

[10]Percival Spear, op. cit., p. 361 fn. 3.
[11]Wm. Theodore de Bary, ed., op. cit., p. 210.

Nor any fatherland do we profess
Except Islam.[12]

B. IQBAL AND ISLAM

Thus as was the case with other Indian thinkers, Iqbal's thought was influenced but not conditioned by the West. Like them, too, he is critical of several aspects of Western culture.[13] Again, like them, he draws inspiration from his own religious tradition—in this case Islamic rather than Hindu. Within Islam it is Sufi tradition that he turns to. He is great admirer of Rumi. However, while he accepts Sufi spirituality, he rejects Sufi quietism.[14] Love of God is a means of inspiration from God rather than mere submission to Him.

> The luminous point whose name is the Self
> Is the life-spark beneath our dust.
> By love it is made more lasting,
> More living, more burning, more glowing.
> From love proceeds the radiance of its being
> And the development of its unknown possibilities.
> Its nature gathers fire from love,
> Love instructs it to illumine the world.
> Love fears neither sword nor dagger,
> Love is not born of water and air and earth.
> Love makes peace and war in the world,
> Love is the fountain of life, love is the flashing
> sword of death,
> The hardest rocks are shivered by love's glance:
> Love of God at last becomes wholly God.[15]

Iqbal also takes a more favourable view of the Mu'tazila, who represented for him the rationalist streak in Islam.[16]

---

[12]Ibid.
[13]Ibid., p. 206.
[14]Ibid., p. 200-201.
[15]Ibid., p. 202.
[16]see Fazlur Rahman, *Islam* (New York: Anchor Books, 1968) p. 271: but also see 277-278.

C. Iqbal And Reinterpretation of Islam

Again like other modern Indian thinkers, although Iqbal respected tradition, this did not prevent him from reinterpreting it. He openly acknowledged the need to do so:

> With the reawakening of Islam, therefore, it is necessary to examine, in an independent spirit, what Europe has thought and how far the conclusions reached by her can help us in the revision and, if necessary, reconstruction, of theological thought in Islam, Besides this is not possible to ignore the generally anti-religious and especially anti-Islamic propaganda in Central Asia which has already crossed the Indian frontier.[17]

One instance of such a reinterpretation may be cited. The doctrine that Muhammad was the "seal of the prophets", i.e. the last prophet, is cardinal to Islam. "The fact that Muhammad is the last in the long chain of messengers is interpreted either in the classical way that this message is valid once for all times, or, as Iqbal has put it, that in Islam prophethood felt the necessity of abolishing itself, thus opening the way to a new kind of scientific Weltanschauung. If true, the second view would grant the Muslims a new approach towards the problems of today." Similarly, it could also be interpreted to mean that henceforth man was on his own and was to guide his own 'evolution', so to say.

D. Remarks

It was shown above how both the Hindu and the Muslim thinkers of the twentieth century in India were influenced by certain common trends, though ironically being subject to the same common trends, in some ways, seems to have led to the growth of separatist tendencies. There is, however, another interesting point of similarity which is not immediately obvious. The main leaders of the Hindu renaissance in the nineteenth

---

[17]Wm. Theodore de Bary, ed., op. cit., p. 207. For more on Iqbal's thought see A. Schimmel, *Gabriel's Wing. A Study of the Religious Ideas of Sir Muhammad Iqbal* (Leiden: E.J. Brill [Numen, spl. 6], 1963).

century seem to have been as often monks as laymen. In the twentieth century, however, the main spokesmen of the Hindu tradition were not monks, even if they possessed an ascetic or reclusive life-style. They were, essentially laymen, even if spiritually inspired. One should note "that the outstanding Muslim writers on the problem of Islam in the modern world, in India as well as the Arabic-speaking world, were nearly all laymen and not theologians." Thus while in the case of the nineteenth century this fact provides a point of contract between the Hindu and Muslim scenes in India, in the context of the twentieth century it provides a point of similarity.

An Overview

In the discussion of religious ferment in the twentieth century
we have so far concentrated on the major religious traditions
in India, namely, Hinduism and Islam and within them on some
of their well-known figures. But this concentration has been
achieved at the expense of range. It is as if we have gazed so
far on the main peaks and the time has come to take a look at
the entire landscape. This result may be achieved through an
overview of the various other forms religious ferment in modern
India assumed.

A. RADICAL HUMANISM

One aspect of the religious ferment in India in the twentieth
century was represented by a trend *against* religion. This was
not an option espoused by many but it did win over at least
one remarkable figure namely, M. N. Roy (1887-1954), whose
original name was Narendranath Bhattacharya.

Ever since the Bolsheviks seized power in Russia in 1917, the
Communists had been eager to link up with the nationalist
movement in India, but the British government was equally keen
to prevent this from happening. Already in 1915, however, the
would-be M. N. Roy had slipped out of India to organize an
armed insurrection against the British. He finally ended up in
Mexico where he heard of the Russian revolution and promptly
helped found a communist party. He then proceeded to Mos-
cow, worked alongside Lenin for a while and became a member
of the Comintern. "Severing his connection with the Comintern

in 1929, Roy returned incognito to India, but was arrested by British authorities and imprisoned for six years. On his release he attempted to organize a non-Stalinist Marxist party within the Indian National Congress. During the Second World War he opposed Gandhi and Nehru, whom he called the tools of Indian Fascism, and supported the Allied Cause. After independence he abandoned Marxism and sought in the secular humanism of Europe the basis of a new social order."[1]

Thus M. N. Roy, who started out as an insurrectionist and then turned into a Marxist, finally ended up as a humanist. But humanism could be rooted in either a secular or a religious world-view. In the case of M. N. Roy it had secular roots, for he "retained from his Communist period a belief in materialism and a deep suspicion of the religious outlook on life, which has played such a dominant role throughout the history of Indian culture."[2]

The case of M.N. Roy illustrates two interesting points. Firstly, it shows that political nationalism *could* be divorced religious nationalism, though this has rarely been the case in India. Secondly, as M. N. Roy "remained an internationalist to the end of his life," Indian nationalism of virtually every type—Hindu, Muslim or Humanist—seems to have been capable of achieving an international dimension.

B. COMMUNISM

The Communist Party of India was founded in 1925[3] and strengthened by the arrival of organizers from Britain in 1926. It was Meerut Conspiracy Case which thrust it into national prominence in 1929. The accused were set free in 1935.

It is interesting to note that at one stage in its evolution the Communist movement in India was nationalist in tone. Nehru was one of the lawyers who defended the accused in the Meerut

[1]Wm. Theodore de Bary, ed., op. cit., p. 354.
[2]Ibid., p. 355.
[3]Amaury de Reincourt, *The Soul of India* (London: Jonathan Cape, 1961) p. 371. Also see R. C. Majumdar, ed., op. cit., p. 421. Groups of Communists had already banded together in 1923 at Calcutta, Bombay, Madras, Lahore and Cawnpore (L. S. S. O'Malley, op. cit., p. 105).

case and Gandhi visited the prisoners in jail.[4] The Meerut case is said to have "placed Communism on a sure footing in India."[5] In its later history, however, the movement took a course at odds with nationalism. "Thus during the period 1930-33, when Gandhi's Civil Disobedience movement swept the country and nationalist movement reached its peak," it has been asserted, "the CPI, instead of joining the fight for freedom, did their best to weaken and sabotage the greatest mass campaign India had so far seen."[6] Later, the Communist Party tried unsuccessfully to infiltrate the Indian National Congress[7] and in 1942 sided with the British in opposition to the national movement.[8]

The history of Communism in India sheds interesting light on the nature of its relation to nationalism. It has been plausibly argued that in countries in which Communism succeeded in allying itself with nationalism, as in China and Viet-Nam it was much more successful than when it was opposed to nationalism—as in India. But if political nationalism in India is rooted in religious nationalism, then the anti-religious stance of Communism should pose problems in the Indian context. There are indications that in the past Communism has sometimes tried to reconcile itself, at least superficially, with religious nationalism by claiming that it followed the "footsteps of the great Indian *rishis* of the glorious past" as much as "of Bolshevik Russia in the modern age."[9]

C. SECULARISM

Humanism and Communism may be regarded as two ideologically profiled forms of secularism if by that expression is meant a movement which reduces the areas of life subject to the influence of religion. Alternatively, and perhaps even simultaneously, it could also mean a state of affairs in which the state is not

[4]Ibid., p. 422, 701.

[5]Ibid , p. 423.

[6]R. C. Majumdar, ed., op. cit., p. 703.

[7]Ibid., p. 703-705.

[8]Ibid., p. 707-708. Also see A. C. Bouquet, *Hinduism* (New York: Hutchinson's University Library, 1948) p. 160.

[9]L. S. S. O'Malley, ed., op. cit., p. 106.

aligned to any religion, as distinguished from a theocracy. There has been a growth of secularism in both these senses in modern India.[10] The concept of a secular state[11] was emphasized to keep political nationalism independent of religious nationalisms. To the extent that India is a secular state this move succeeded; to the extent that Pakistan is not, it failed.

Secularism in both these aspects is associated with the name of Jawaharlal Nehru (d. 1964), independent India's first prime-minister.[12] It is worth noting, however, that the concept of a secular state seems to have had a religious underpinning in the Indian context, as both Gandhi and Nehru opted for it. "Gandhi's starting point was that of a religious man who, believing all religions to be true, accepted a theory of the state which fit in with this belief; hence the secular state. Nehru's starting point was that of a practical political thinker and leader who, while personally believing all religions to be mostly untrue, had to provide for their freedom to function peacefully without prejudicing the democratic system; hence the secular state."[13]

D. BUDDHISM

The formation of the Mahabodhi Society by Anagarika Dharmapala was referred to in Part One of the book. One factor in the religious ferment in modern India, it was mentioned earlier, was orientalism. In the case of Buddhism in India it was this aspect which became prominent in the twentieth century, perhaps because there were hardly any Buddhists as such to provide a demographic base for the expression of religious or political nationalism. This phase, which Adele M. Fiske has called the "second period" in the history of the Mahabodhi Society "was

[10]Donald Smith, *India as a Secular State* (Princeton University Press, 1963) passim; Beatrice Pitney Lamb, *India A World in Transition* (New York: Frederick A. Praeger, 1963) p. 199, 309, etc.

[11]R. I. Crane, ed., op. cit., p. 314-315, etc. Ironically, it has also gone hand in hand with rise in communalism (see Beatrice Pitney Lamb, op. cit., p. 247).

[12]Beatrice Pitney Lamb, op. cit., p. 202, 309.

[13]Donald E. Smith, *Nehru and Democracy: The Political Thought of an Asian Democrat* (Calcutta: Orient Longmans, 1958) p. 156.

marked by the coming to the Society of three young Indian intellectuals, former members of the Arya Samaj—Anand Kausalyayana of the Punjab, Jagadish Kashyap of Bihar, and Rahul Sankrityayan of Uttar Pradesh . . . The three began a work of collecting, editing and translating Pali texts, work that gave new scholarly distinction to the Society."[14]

It is the work of Dr B.R. Ambedkar among the Mahars which represents the missionary forces released in Buddhism in the context of religious ferment in modern India. Dr. Ambedkar was a leader of the untouchables who was not happy with the Gandhian solution to their problems.[15] He had concluded by 1935 that the untouchables could not hope to find justice within Hinduism; however, if they converted to Islam or Christianity they ran the risk of becoming 'denationalised'.[16] Hence in 1956 he offered conversion to Buddhism as a way out of their predicament and "within two years after his conversion, the Neo-Buddhist population was 18 to 20 million."[17]

E. JAINISM

In 1947 India had more Jains than Buddhists. According to the Census, there were 1.6 million Jains in India in 1951. According to a seasoned observer of the Indian religious scene, "In the last hundred years the Jains of India, one of the wealthiest and best-educated communities of the subcontinent, have maintained their solidarity and have tried to adapt their doctrines to modern needs and conditions. A good deal of money and labor has been spent on propaganda, not only to prevent younger members of the community from succumbing to the temptations of twentieth-century materialism, but also to ob-

[14]Heinrich Dumoulin, ed., *Buddhism in the Modern World* (London: Collier Macmillan Publishers, 1976) p. 131.

[15]B. R. Ambedkar, *What Congress and Gandhi Have Done to the Untouchables* (Bombay: Thacker and Co., 1945).

[16]He did not opt for Sikhism or Jainism perhaps because one was too militant and the other not at all. See T. S. Wilkinson and M. M. Thomas, eds., *Ambedkar and the Neo-Buddhist Movement* (Bangalore: The Christian Institute for the Study of Religion and Society, 1972) p. 58.

[17]Ibid., p. 32.

tain sympathizers, and even converts, from other communities. Among the most active Jain propagandists was the late Mr. Champat Rai Jain, an able barrister with a good command of English, Hindi, and Urdu, and a wide knowledge of his own and other religions, who devoted many years with self-sacrificing whole-heartedness to writing and speaking in favor of Jainism."[18]

Thus religious ferment in modern India also seems to have affected Jainism much the same way as it had affected other religions in India.

F. SIKHISM

Sikhism provides an interesting illustration of religious ferment in modern India in its double aspect of releasing forces represented by religious and political nationalism.

The rise of political nationalism among the Sikhs is of special interest as they had remained loyal to the British even during the rebellion of 1857. Towards the end of the nineteenth century the Sikhs started getting organized, a process culminating in the formation of the Chief Khalsa Diwan. The Sikhs, now organized, clashed with the British government in a major way during two periods: from 1912-19 and 1920-25. On the first occasion it was the Government's efforts to acquire land belonging to the Gurdwara Rikab Ganj to widen a road in connection with the construction of the new capital at Delhi. The Government backed down in 1919 in the face of agitation. The second clash was precipitated by the efforts of the Sikhs to exercise full control over their own religious institutions and Gurdwaras. The Akalis, 'a body of Puritan Sikhs', led the movement and after an unsuccessful effort on the part of the Government to suppress the movement, a compromise was negotiated in the form of the Gurdwara Bill of 1925. It was further amended in 1945.[19] "Thus the history of the Sikhs resembles to a large extent that of the Hindus, and illustrates the tendency of the religious bodies to shed the purely religious aspect and to

---

[18]Wm. Theodore de Bary, ed., op. cit., Vol. I, p. 80.
[19]R. C. Majumdar, ed., op. cit., p. 990.

assume more or less the character of a nationalist and political party."[20]

The rise of Sikh nationalism can also be compared to the rise of Muslim nationalism in at least two ways. It also resulted in a somewhat muffled demand for an independent Sikh state and it led to a sense of separateness on the part of the Sikhs from the Hindus. But while with the Muslims the Hindu claim was that the Muslims are Indians and therefore should continue to be a part of an undivided India, with regard to the Sikhs the Hindu claim is that they are Hindus. Many Sikhs challenge this identification.[21]

G. Islam

The religious ferment in India was also reflected in the world of Indian Islam. Mention has already been made of the All-India Muslim League and its contribution to the achievement of Pakistan. The Muslim League was an expression of political nationalism as an off-shoot of religious nationalism. This movement for Pakistan is associated with the so-called Aligarh movement. It takes its name from the Islamic educational institutions founded at Aligarh in 1875 at the instance of Sir Syed Khan (1817—1898) with British support.[22] But no discussion of Indian Islam can be complete without a reference to the Deoband school. This school was set up in 1867 by "Muslim intellectuals and national leaders who had taken a prominent part in the Indian revolt of 1857."[23] After the start of the Aligarh movement there commenced a great rivalry between the two. "Whilst the orthodox movement, attempting to resuscitate classical Islam, was intensely opposed to British rule in India, the unorthodox movement seeking to carve a new image of Islam, advocated loyalty to British power. The orthodox saw the security of Islam in a free and united India. The unorthodox, fearful of Hindu supremacy, eventually sought the partition

[20]Ibid., p. 991.

[21]Ibid.

[22]See K. M. Panikkar, op. cit., Chapter XXII.

[23]D. P. Singhal, *India and World Civilization* (London: Sidgwick and Jackson, 1972) p. 289.

of the country."[24]

Maulana Abul Kalam Azad (1818-1958) may be seen as continuing the Deoband tradition. He was an important leader of the Indian National Congress. "Although educated entirely in the orthodox tradition, he imbibed the spirit of the modern West" and "interpreted Islam as a universal religion which could embrace the diversity of all creeds."[25]

Another school which needs to be mentioned is the Nadwatu'l-'Ulema (the Association of Ulemas) of Lucknow, which under the leadership of Maulana Shibli (1857-1914) "stood between the ultra-modernism of Aligarh and extreme orthodoxy of Deoband."[26]

Finally, the links of religious nationalism in Islam with the international situation need to be noted. Unlike Hinduism, Islam is a global religion. This imparted to it an international character which found expression in the Khilafat campaign and the pan-Islamism of Iqbal.

The general state of Islam during the period under review may be summed up as follows. The "political, economic, and moral decline of the Muslims continued to engage the minds of their leaders from 1905 to 1947. They tried to determine its causes and remove them. But the problem is difficult and complicated and involves the question of values. There is bound to be serious difference of opinion among the leaders about it. The Aligarh movement attached the greatest importance to the economic aspect of the problem. The Deoband school ignored this aspect and attached greater value to its moral and political aspect. The Nadwatu'l-'Ulema ignored the political aspect and tried to bridge the gulf between the Aligarh and the Deoband schools of thought. The Khaksar emphasized the physical and moral discipline. The Tablighi Jamà'at attached the greatest value to the religious and moral aspect of the problem and ignored all the other aspects entirely. Dr. Iqbal gave the importance to all the aspects of the problem and suggested the remedy for all of them. He wanted the establishment of a model State in

[24]Ibid., p. 291.
[25]On his significance for Islam in India see Kenneth Cragg, op. cit., p. 121.
[26]R. C. Majumdar, ed., op. cit., p. 1070.

which all the spiritual and physical urges of man might be satisfied and no individual or group was exploited by another. But
it remained only an ideal."[27]

H. HINDUISM

The discussion of new figures and forces operating in Hinduism
should not obscure the fact that movements within Hinduism
discussed in the first part of the book also continued to be factors in the Hindu situation. The Arya Samaj and the Ramakrishna Mission continued to grow in influence; the Brahmo
Samaj, the Prarthana Samaj and the Theosophical Society perhaps less so. What is more, apart from the various figures and
forces already discussed, religious ferment in Hinduism covered
a wider spectrum. We must now take a brief look at these
other movements not discussed hitherto.

The Hindu figures discussed in Part Two—namely Rabindranath Tagore, Aurobindo Ghosh and Mahatma Gandhi may be
said to represent the liberal tradition of Hinduism. Under
Gandhi's leadership the Indian National Congress sought to
become the political expression of both liberal Hinduism and
liberal Islam. But on its flanks arose movements which were
more conservative in nature. The Muslim League represented
Islamic political conservatism, Hindu conservatism found an
expression through the Hindu Mahasabha.[28] "The Hindu
Mahasabha, a definitely communal organisation of the Hindus,
was undoubtedly brought into existence as a counter-poise to
the All-India Muslim League, the communal organisation of
the Muslims."[29] The "genesis and early history"of the Hindu
Mahasabha "are somewhat obscure", but it came into being
through a series of steps first taken in 1910. It may be said to
have emerged by 1918. The Moplah rebellion of 1921,[30] which
involved Muslim attacks on the Hindus of Malabar, brought it
into prominence and its best known leaders Madan Mohan
Malaviya and V. D. Savarkar encouraged the move towards

[27]Ibid., p. 1073.
[28]L. S. S. O'Malley, ed., op. cit., p. 761.
[29]R. C. Majumdar, ed., *Struggle for Freedom,* p. 419.
[30]Ibid., p. 360ff.

Hindu Sangathan or Hindu solidarity. The Hindu Mahasabha also worked to safeguard the political rights of the Hindus vis-a-vis the Muslims, reconverted several Muslims to Hinduism and also emphasized the need to remove such abuses from Hindu society as child marriage, casteism, untouchability, etc. But it "gradually distinguished itself more by political than social or religious activities."[31] In the opinion of many scholars the activities of the Hindu Mahasabha served to alienate the Muslims.[32]

Another Hindu movement, which emphasized Hindu cultural solidarity, was started in 1925 by Dr. K. S. Hedgewar (1889—1940).[33] It is known as the Rashtriya Swayamsevek Sangh or RSS for short. "Individual members of the group were much more at home ideologically with the Hindu Mahasabhā than with the party of Gāndhī and Nehru, and undoubtedly gave the former more direct political support. With the coming of freedom, accompanied as it was by the partition and the resulting holocaust of mass migration and refugee resettlement, the RSS quickly became identified with extreme Hindu nationalist sentiment."[34]

Mention must also be made of the different non-Brahmin organizations in South India which were formed to protest against Brahmin dominance. In 1924 they merged to form All-India Non-Brahmin Conference.[35] Its chief leader was A. Ramaswami Mudaliar. It was a political organization with a communal character.[36] The formation of such a group is an indication of the anti-casteist character of much of the religious ferment in modern India, though ironically one effect of the ferment may have been to strengthen caste organizations.

[31]Ibid., p. 420.
[32]Wm. Theodore de Bary, ed., op. cit., p. 281; R. I. Crane, ed., op. cit., p. 309; etc.
[33]Philip H. Ashby, *Modern Trends in Hinduism* (New York: Columbia University Press, 1974) p. 99.
[34]Ibid., p. 100.
[35]R. C. Majumdar, ed., op. cit., p. 420.
[36]Ibid., p. 421.

Finally it must be pointed out that many men and movements representing and participating in the religious and political ferment must only be referred to here in passing, or not at all in this part of the book, such as Mrs. Annie Besant, Dr. S. Radhakrishnan, the Deva Samaj, the Zoroastrians, etc.

Name and Author Index

Subject Index

Word Index